United States Nuclear Regulatory Commission

Protecting People and the Environment

ENFORCEMENT PRO GRAM
ANNUAL REPORT
Calendar Year 2011

U.S. Nuclear Regulatory Commission
Office of Enforcement
Washington, DC 20555

Contents

- TABLES –

- FIGURES -

- APPENDICES -

Executive Summary

The U.S. Nuclear Regulatory Commission (NRC) effectively implemented the Enforcement Policy and Program in Calendar Year (CY) 2011. The relevant NRC Headquarters offices and regional offices continued to focus on appropriate and consistent enforcement of the agency's regulations.

Escalated Enforcement Action Data

In CY 2011, the agency issued 96 escalated enforcement actions, which included 14 actions involving civil penalties totaling $146,750 and 82 escalated notices of violation without a civil penalty. No civil penalties were assessed against reactor facilities in CY 2011. Five of the 14 actions involving civil penalties totaling $50,000 were confirmatory orders issued as a result of successful mediation sessions conducted through the agency's Alternative Dispute Resolution (ADR) Program. In addition, the NRC issued five enforcement orders in CY 2011, including a prohibition of an individual from involvement in NRC-licensed activities and an order to suspend a license. The number of escalated enforcement actions without civil penalties is consistent with that of previous years and is equal to the 5-year average. The total number of escalated enforcement actions decreased in CY 2011 largely because of a decrease in the number of enforcement actions related to civil penalties. Although the number and monetary amount of civil penalties in CY 2011 decreased from CY 2010 levels, these values are comparable to the number of civil penalties the agency issued in CY 2009. Of the 96 escalated enforcement actions issued in CY 2011, the agency withheld 35 from the public because they involved security or safeguards violations.

Noteworthy Program Accomplishments

The Office of Enforcement (OE) issued two Interim Enforcement Policy guidance documents and seven Enforcement Guidance Memoranda to give the staff and outside stakeholders information on the dispositioning of specific enforcement actions. In addition, OE assessed implementation of the agency's enforcement program at two regions in CY 2011. The agency continued the successful use of the ADR Program in nine enforcement cases.

Significant Cases

In CY 2011, the agency processed a number of significant cases that required extensive coordination and cooperation between internal and external stakeholders. These significant cases included: (1) a Severity Level III violation issued to the U.S. Department of the Army, (2) a notice of violation associated with a red significance determination process finding issued to Browns Ferry Nuclear Power Plant, (3) a notice of violation associated with a yellow significance determination process finding issued to Oconee Nuclear Station, and (4) an Atomic Safety and Licensing Board (ASLB) order that the agency issued after it successfully reached settlement agreements in prehearing negotiations with Mattingly Testing Services.

I. Program Overview

A. Mission and Authority

The U.S. Nuclear Regulatory Commission (NRC) regulates the civilian uses of nuclear materials in the United States to protect public health and safety, the environment, and the common defense and security. The agency accomplishes this mission through: licensing of nuclear facilities and the possession, use, and disposal of nuclear materials; the development and implementation of requirements governing licensed activities; and inspection and enforcement activities to ensure compliance with these requirements.

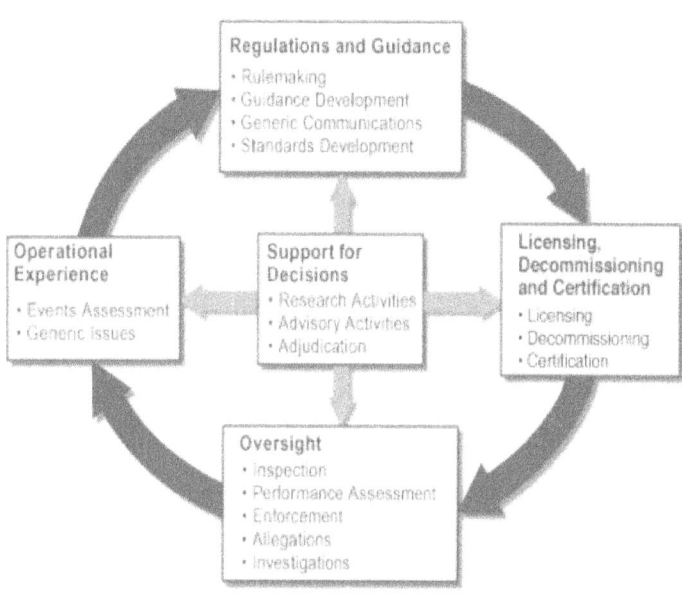

Figure 1: How the NRC Regulates

The NRC conducts various types of inspections and investigations designed to ensure that the activities it licenses are conducted in strict compliance with the Commission's regulations, the terms of the licenses, and other requirements.

The sources of the NRC's enforcement authority are the Atomic Energy Act of 1954, as amended, the Energy Reorganization Act of 1974, as amended, and the Energy Policy Act of 2005. These statutes give the NRC broad authority. The Energy Policy Act of 2005 expanded the definition of byproduct material, placing additional byproduct material under the NRC's jurisdiction including both naturally occurring and accelerator-produced radioactive materials (NARM). The agency implements its enforcement authority through Title 10 of the Code of Federal Regulations (10 CFR) Part 2, "Rules of Practice for Domestic Licensing Proceedings and Issuance of Orders," Subpart B, "Procedures for Imposing Requirements by Order, or for Modification, Suspension, or Revocation of a License, or for Imposing Civil Penalties." The Administrative Dispute Resolution Act of 1996 provides the statutory framework for the Federal Government to use alternative dispute resolution (ADR).

The NRC Enforcement Policy establishes the general principles governing the NRC's Enforcement Program and specifies a process for implementing the agency's enforcement authority in response to violations of NRC requirements. This statement of policy is predicated on the NRC's view that compliance with NRC requirements serves a key role in ensuring safety, maintaining security, and protecting the environment. The Enforcement Policy applies to all NRC licensees, to various categories of nonlicensees, and to individual employees of licensed and nonlicensed firms involved in NRC-regulated activities.

The NRC enforces compliance as necessary. Enforcement actions serve as a deterrent, emphasize the importance of compliance with regulatory requirements, and encourage prompt identification and prompt, comprehensive correction of violations. In addition, because violations occur in a variety of activities and have varying levels of significance, the NRC Enforcement Policy contains graduated sanctions.

Enforcement authority includes the use of notices of violation, civil penalties, demands for information, and orders to modify, suspend, or revoke a license. The NRC staff may exercise discretion in determining the appropriate enforcement sanctions to be taken. Most violations are identified through inspections and investigations and are normally assigned a severity level (SL) ranging from SL IV for those of more than minor concern to SL I for the most significant.

The Reactor Oversight Process (ROP) supplements the enforcement process for operating nuclear reactors. Under the ROP, violations are not normally assigned a severity level but instead are assessed through the ROP and usually referred to as "findings." Under this program, the NRC determines the risk significance of inspection findings using the significance determination process (SDP), which assigns the colors of green, white, yellow, or red with increasing risk significance. Findings under the ROP may also include licensee failures to meet self-imposed standards. As such, an ROP finding may or may not involve a violation of a regulatory requirement. While the ROP can process most violations at operating power reactors, it cannot address aspects of some violations; such violations require the NRC to follow the traditional enforcement process.

These violations include violations that resulted in actual safety or security consequences, violations that may affect the ability of the NRC to perform its regulatory oversight function, and violations that involve willfulness. In addition, while ROP findings are not normally subject to civil penalties, the NRC does consider civil penalties for any violation that involves actual consequences. SL IV violations and violations associated with green ROP findings are normally dispositioned as noncited violations (NCVs). Inspection reports or inspection records document NCVs and briefly describe the corrective action that the licensee has taken or plans to take, if known at the time the NCV is documented. Additional information about the ROP is available at http://www.nrc.gov/NRR/OVERSIGHT/ASSESS/index.html.

OE develops policies and programs for the enforcement of NRC requirements. In addition, OE oversees NRC enforcement, giving programmatic and implementation direction to regional and Headquarters offices that conduct or are involved in enforcement activities, and ensures that regional and program offices consistently implement the agency's enforcement program.

The Director of OE reports directly to the Deputy Executive Director for Materials, Waste, Research, State, Tribal, and Compliance Programs (DEDMRT), and is responsible for ensuring that the DEDMRT is kept apprised of certain escalated actions. The DEDMRT is consulted in any case that involves novel issues; substantial legal, programmatic, or policy issues raised during the enforcement review process; or in any case in which the Director of OE believes the DEDMRT's involvement is warranted. OE works in partnership with NRC Headquarters and regional offices to enforce the agency's requirements.

The NRC's enforcement Web site (http://www.nrc.gov/about-nrc/regulatory/enforcement.html) presents a variety of information, such as the Enforcement Policy; the Enforcement Manual; and current temporary enforcement guidance contained in enforcement guidance memoranda. This Web site also has information about significant enforcement actions the NRC has issued to reactor and materials licensees, nonlicensees (vendors, contractors, and certificate holders), and individuals. Consistent with NRC practices and policies, most security-related actions and activities are not available on the NRC's public Web site. However, OE's collection of enforcement documents includes security orders that impose compensatory security requirements on various licensees.

In addition to enforcement activities, OE's oversight responsibilities include, in part, the Allegations Program, Employee Protection and Discrimination, and the ADR Program (both early-ADR and post-investigation ADR). More information about OE's responsibilities is available on the NRC's public Web site at http://www.nrc.gov/about-nrc/organization/oefuncdesc.html.

B. Assessment of Escalated Enforcement Actions

Escalated enforcement actions include the following:

- notices of violations (NOVs) including SL I, II, or III violations
- NOVs associated with red, yellow, or white SDP findings (for ope ating reactor facilities)
- civil penalty actions
- orders (including confirmatory orders that result from the ADR process)

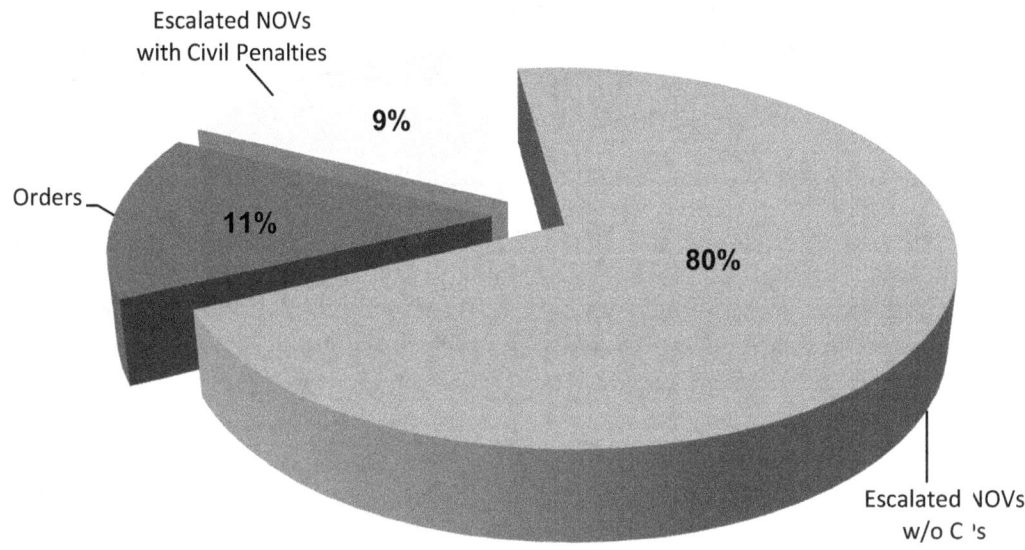

Figure 2: Escalated Enforcement by Type of Enforcement Action

Figure 2 (above) shows the distribution of escalated enforcement actions t ie NRC issued in Calendar Year (CY) 2011 by type of action for the 96 total action ; issued throughout the year to all licensees. The most common escalated enforce nent action was an NOV without a civil penalty. Table 1 (below) shows that the agenc / issued 77 NOVs without a civil penalty in CY 2011. According to the Enforcement Policy, Section 2.3.4, civil penalties may not be warranted if a licensee takes adequate corrective action to prevent recurrence of an identified SL III violation. Generally speaking, the large percentage of NOVs without civil penalties is considered a positive trend because it reflects a strong licensee program with the majority of licensees adequately responding to escalated enforcement actions. Nine of the NO 's and five of the ADR orders issued in CY 2011 included a civil penalty. Although the total number of escalated enforcement actions with a civil penalty is less than the number issued in CY 2010, it is approximately equivalent to the number issued in Y 2009, CY 2007, and CY 2006. The five ADR orders issued with civil penalties reflect a significant increase in the issuance of civil penalties associated with enforcement mediation activities. In previous years, the NRC issued only one ADR order with a civil penalty. Including the ADR orders with civil penalties, there were 10 actions involved the issuance of an order. This is a decrease from the 17 orders issued in CY 2010 and is below the 5-year average.

Figure 3 (below) shows the distribution of enforcement actions based on the types of licensees to whom the NRC issued escalated enforcement actions were issued in CY 2011. For this chart, individual actions were included in the appropriate category of licensee, instead of being counted separately. The following charts and the tables at the end of this report give further detail by identifying the region or program office that initiated the action, as well as the licensees, nonlicensees, and individuals involved.

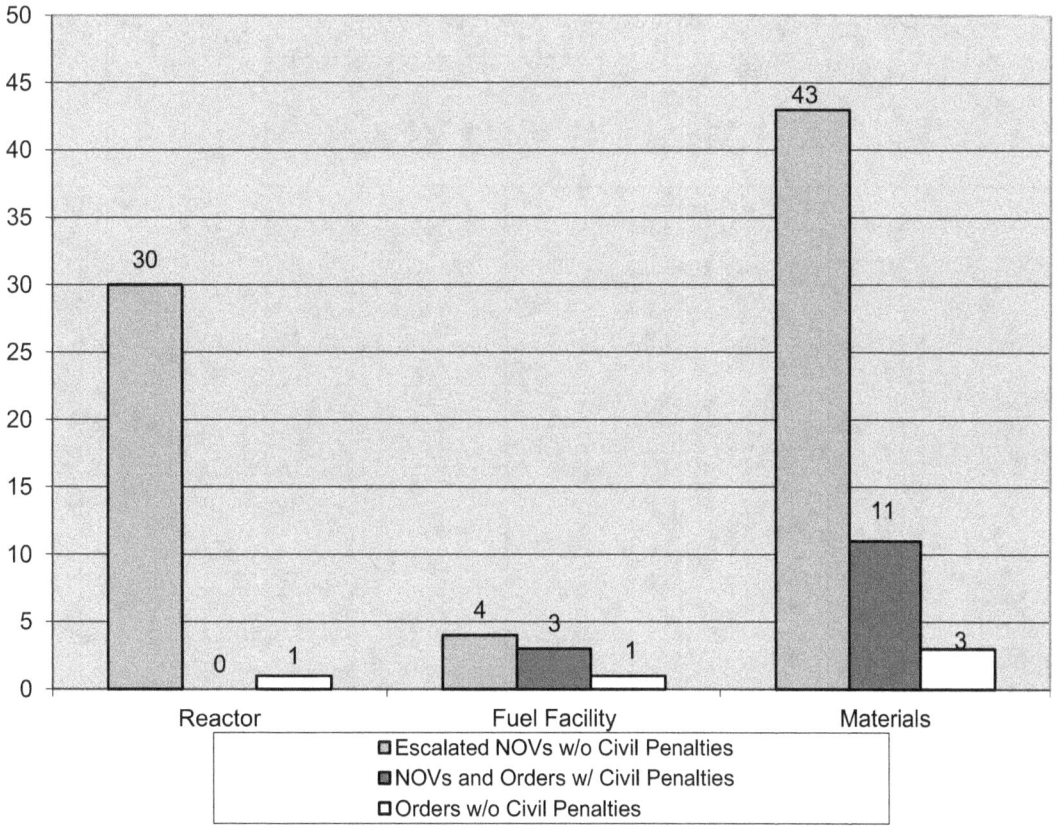

Figure 3: Escalated Enforcement by Type of Licensee

The larger number of escalated enforcement actions issued to materials licensees reflects the significantly larger number of materials licenses (approximately 3,000) when compared to licenses for operating reactors (104) and fuel facilities (13). The majority of escalated enforcement actions issued to materials licensees without civil penalties were issued for gauge users and hospitals, as shown in Table 4. This is consistent with the distribution of escalated enforcement actions issued to materials licensees in past years and reflects the increased emphasis on inspections for security and control of licensed materials. The number of escalated enforcement actions associated with reactor facilities in CY 2011 is relatively consistent with that of past years; however, CY 2011 saw a noticeable decrease in the number of escalated enforcement actions associated with materials licensees (25 percent) from CY 2010. This decrease may be attributable to three states (New Jersey, Pennsylvania, and Virginia) achieving agreement state status in the past few years. The 57 escalated enforcement actions are comparable to the number of actions issued in CY 2006. The NRC will evaluate this trend in the future. The total number of escalated enforcement actions issued to fuel cycle facilities decreased, but is comparable to that of CY 2010.

1.   Escalated Enforcement Trends

In CY 2011, the agency issued 96 escalated enforcement actions. Although this number is a 22 percent decrease from that of CY 2010, the 96 escalated enforcement actions are comparable to the number of actions issued in CY 2006. The NRC will evaluate this trend in the future. Table 1 shows a breakdown of the number of escalated enforcement actions from CY 2006 to CY 2011 by type of enforcement action. Figure 4 displays this information in graphical form.

Table 1 – Escalated Action Trends

	CY 2011	CY 2010	CY 2009	CY 2008	CY 2007	CY 2006	Average
Escalated NOVs (w/o CPs)	77	84	76	94	77	57	78
NOVs and Orders w/CPs	14	24	17	28	18	15	19
Orders (w/o CPs)	5	15	25	35	22	15	20
Orders Imposing CPs	0	1	3	0	1	0	1
Total	96	124	121	157	118	87	117

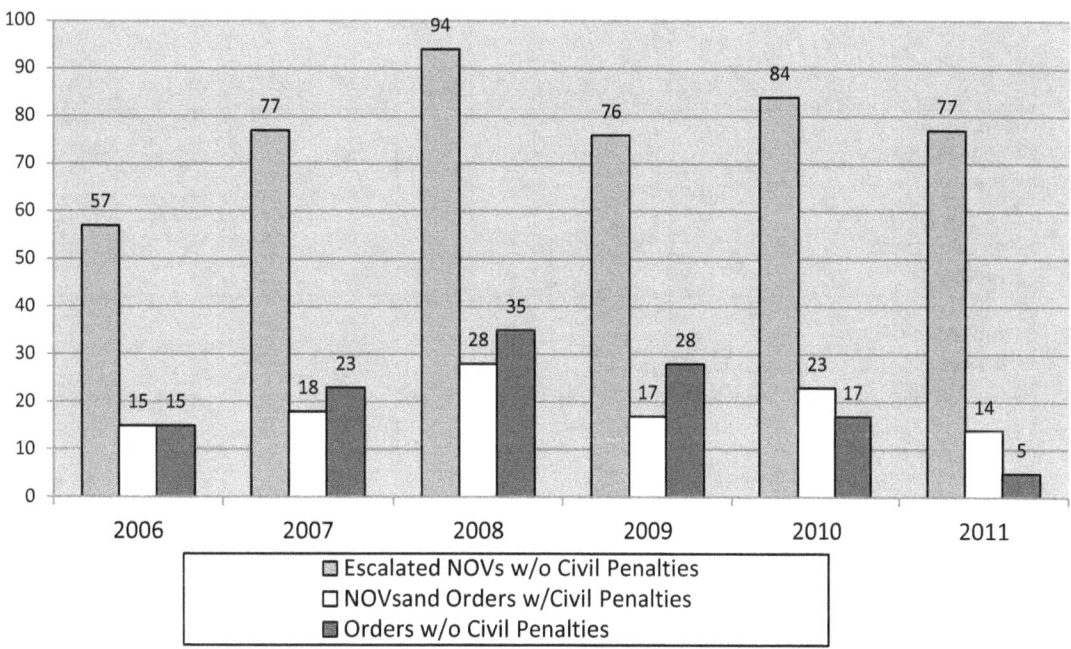

Figure 4: Escalated Action Trends (CY 2006—CY 2011)

As shown in Table 1 above, the total number of escalated enforcement actions issued in 2011 is less than the 6-year average. The number of enforcement actions not associated with a civil penalty is consistent with the 6-year average. The number of enforcement actions associated with civil penalties, although smaller than in previous years, is comparable to the 6-year average. Table 1 shows a noticeable declining trend in the issuance of orders not associated with civil penalties. This is cause, in part, by the maturation of the ADR Program and the increased use of civil penalties in the mediation process.

2.   Civil Penalty Actions

In CY 2011, the agency processed 14 cases that involved civil penalties. Five of the 14 cases were associated with ADR settlements following successful mediation sessions. This number represents a significant increase over previous years in which no more than one ADR order involved a civil penalty.

Nine of these cases involved willfulness which is defined as either deliberate misconduct or careless disregard. The Commission is particularly concerned with the identification of willful violations. The NRC's regulatory program is based on licensees and their contractors, employees, and agents acting with integrity and communicating with candor; therefore, the agency may consider a violation involving willfulness to be more egregious than the underlying violation, taken alone, would have been, and it may increase the severity level accordingly.

Table 2 – Civil Penalty Information

	CY 2011	CY 2010	CY 2009	CY 2008	CY 2007	CY 2006	Average
Number of Proposed Civil Penalties	14	23	17	28	18	15	**19**
Number of Orders that Imposed Civil Penalties	0	1	3	0	1	0	**1**
Number of Civil Penalties Paid	11	21	15	29	17	16	**18**
Amount of Proposed Civil Penalties	$146,750	$673,700	$174,000	$1,185,900	$383,200	$332,350	**$482,650**
Amount of Imposed Civil Penalties[1]	$0	$32,500	$29,250	$0	$3,250	$0	**$10,833**
Amount of Civil Penalties Paid	$123,529	$639,480	$279,750	$1,039,850	$446,500	$375,500	**$484,102**

Table 2 compares civil penalty assessments proposed, imposed, and paid for the current calendar year to those of the previous five years and the 6-year average. When reviewing the information in this table, it is important to note that an enforcement action may include more than one civil penalty or more than one violation. In addition, a civil penalty may be proposed in one year and paid or imposed in another year. In some cases, the NRC has approved a civil penalty payment plan whereby a licensee is permitted to pay the civil penalty in regular installments. Finally, the amount of a proposed civil penalty may be reduced, for example, as a result of exercising discretion as part of a settlement agreement developed during ADR.

The total number of civil penalties proposed in CY 2011 decreased from the number proposed in CY 2010 and is below the average number proposed over the last six years. No civil penalties were assessed against reactor facilities in CY 2011. The total dollar amount of proposed civil penalties decreased significantly in CY 2011 compared with CY 2010, mainly as a result of the civil penalties issued in CY 2010 to the U.S. Department of Veterans Affairs (VA) Philadelphia Medical Center, Nuclear Fuel Services (NFS), and Florida Power and Light's Turkey Point Plant. The amount of civil penalties proposed in CY 2011 is comparable to the amount proposed in CY 2009.

---

[1] The NRC issues an "order imposing civil monetary penalty" when a licensee chooses not to pay a proposed civil penalty, unless a basis exists for withdrawal of the proposed penalty.

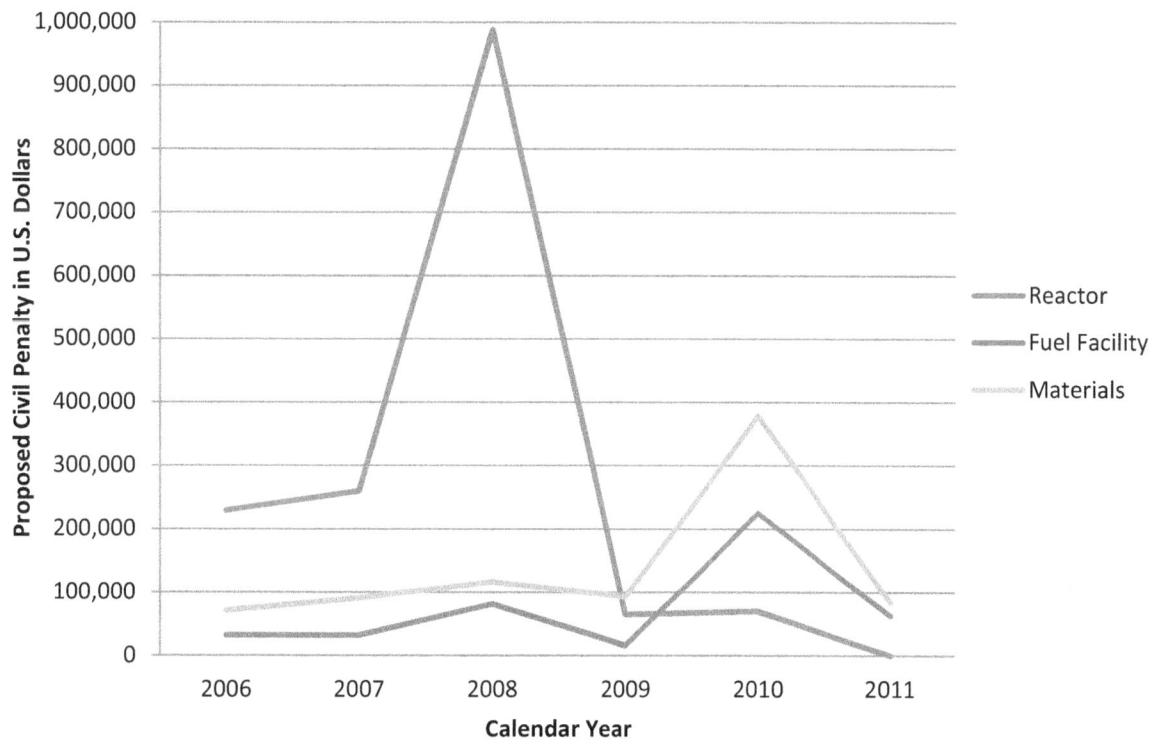

**Figure 5: Comparison of Amount of Proposed
Civil Penalties (in U.S. Dollars) by Licensee Type for CY 2006—2011**

Figures 5 (above) shows the dollar amount of civil penalties proposed for reactor, materials, and fuel facility licensees in CY 2011 and the preceding five years. Figure 6 (below) shows a significant increase in the percentage of the total civil penalty amount issued to fuel cycle and materials licensees in CY 2011. This is because no civil penalties were issued to reactor licensees in CY 2011. The largest peaks are frequently the result of a single civil penalty (e.g., Indian Point Nuclear Station in 2008 and the Philadelphia VA Medical Center in 2010). As a consequence, a single year may not indicate a trend—an important factor to consider in assessing possible trends.

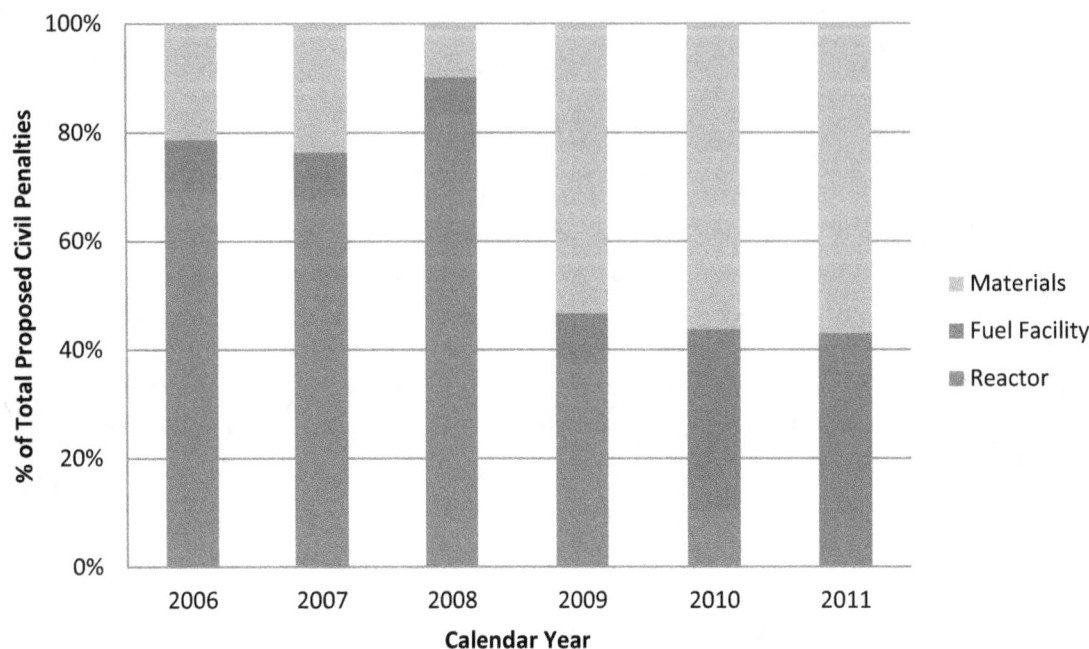

**Figure 6: Percentage of Proposed Civil Penalties
by Licensee Type for CY 2006—2011**

Appendix A to this report includes a brief description of each of the civil penalty actions for CY 2011. Security related issues involving NOVs with civil penalties are not addressed in Appendix A; however, the number of NOVs associated with security related issues is included in the data discussed in this report.

3.   Notices of Violation without Civil Penalties

In accordance with Section 2.3.4 of the Enforcement Policy, a civil penalty may not be warranted for escalated enforcement actions if certain criteria are met. For instance, (1) the identified violation is the first non-willful SL III violation identified in the past two years or two inspections at the licensee's facility and the licensee took adequate corrective action to prevent its recurrence, or (2) this was not the first non-willful SL III violation identified in the past two years or two inspections, but the licensee self-identified the violation and took adequate corrective action to prevent its recurrence. In addition, the agency may use enforcement discretion, when deemed appropriate, to refrain from proposing a civil penalty, regardless of the normal civil penalty assessment process described above.

In CY 2011, the NRC issued 77 escalated NOVs without civil penalties. Of these violations, 24 were associated with white SDP findings under the ROP. One violation was associated with a yellow SDP finding, and one violation was associated with a red SDP finding. The NRC issued five NOVs associated with green SDP findings to reactor licensees. NOVs associated with green SDP findings are not considered escalated enforcement actions.

Appendix B to this report summarizes each of these NOVs without civil penalties issued to licensees, as well as the NOVs associated with SDP findings. Security related issues involving NOVs without civil penalties are not addressed in Appendix B; however, the number of NOVs associated with security related issues is included in the data discussed in this report.

4. Alternative Dispute Resolution (ADR)

The term "post-investigation ADR" refers to the use of mediation after the NRC Office of Investigations (OI) has completed its investigation and an enforcement panel has concluded that pursuit of an enforcement action appears to be warranted. Under the NRC's post-investigation ADR process, mediation may be offered at three points in the enforcement process for discrimination and other wrongdoing cases: (1) before a predecisional enforcement conference; (2) after the initial enforcement action is taken, typically the issuance of an NOV; or (3) after cases result in the issuance of an order imposing a civil penalty, but before a hearing request. Mediation is an informal and voluntary process in which a neutral mediator with no decision-making authority helps the parties attempt to reach an agreement. The staff believes that for certain escalated enforcement actions mediation affords the staff an opportunity to institute broader or more comprehensive corrective actions to better ensure public health and safety than outcomes typically achieved through the traditional enforcement process.

As Figure 7 shows, the number of confirmatory orders arising from the post-investigation ADR program generally stayed at the same typical levels of approximately 5 to 10 confirmatory orders per year (excluding the uncharacteristically high number in CY 2009). In CY 2011, the NRC participated in seven post-investigation ADR mediations that resulted in orders confirming the terms of the parties' agreement (one reactor licensee and six materials licensees).

In CY 2011, the staff continued its focus on enhancing the post-investigation ADR program's timeliness, transparency and overall effectiveness by implementing several initiatives. Those initiatives included (1) holding a public meeting to solicit feedback from the program's public stakeholders; (2) redesigning the program's public Web page, thereby making more information available; (3) revising several program documents, such as the post-investigation brochure; and, (4) issuing more internal and external guidance documents. Although the realization of the impact of the NRC's ADR initiatives is more evolutionary than instantaneous, the timeliness data (Figure 8) reflects a positive trend.

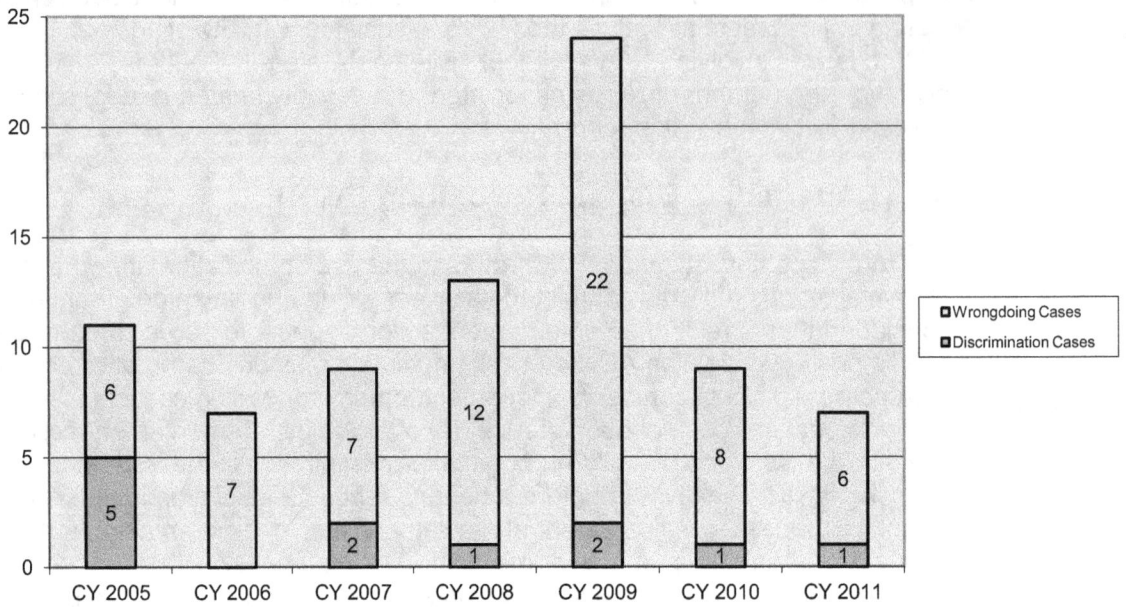

Figure 7: ADR Confirmatory Orders Issued in CY 2005—2011

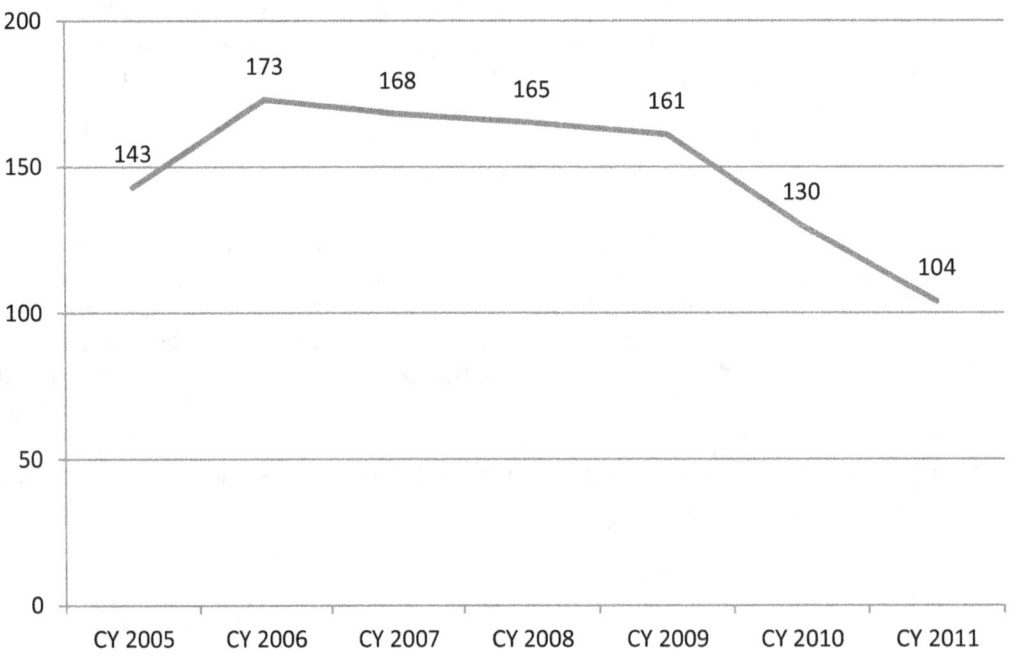

Figure 8: Calendar Days from NRC Action to Issuance of Confirmatory Order

II. Enforcement Case Work

A. Significant Enforcement Actions

In CY 2011, the agency was involved in several significant enforcement actions that required coordination among internal and external stakeholders beyond the typical enforcement case and were noteworthy in some aspects.

U.S. Department of the Army—U.S. Army Installation Management Command

On August 1, 2011, an NOV was issued to the U.S. Department of the Army (Army) for a violation associated with possession of depleted uranium (DU) without an NRC license following the expiration of its associated license in April 1978. The Army continued to possess DU, in the form of spent fragments of spotting rounds (obtained from 1962 to 1968, and expended before 1968), at firing ranges located at the Army's two Hawaiian installations, Schofield Barracks and Pohakuloa Training Area; as well as other installations across the United States.

This violation of 10 CFR 40.3, "License Requirements," which states, in part, that persons may not receive title to own, receive, possess, use, transfer, or dispose of source material unless authorized in a specific or general license issued by the NRC, was categorized at Severity Level III in accordance with the Enforcement Policy. The NRC considered this violation significant because the requirements in 10 CFR 40.3 give reasonable assurance that control of radioactive material will be adequate to prevent unauthorized removal or access, and to ensure that exposures to workers, members of the public, and the environment do not exceed NRC dose limits.

On April 4, 2011, the NRC conducted a meeting with the Army Installation Management Command staff, to discuss the basis for the violation. The NRC also described the violation in detail in a letter to the Army dated April 5, 2011 (Agencywide Documents Access and management System (ADAMS) Accession No. ML110660245. A public predecisional enforcement conference with the Army was held on May 10, 2011, in the NRC's Region IV offices to give the Army an opportunity to present its perspective on the violation before the NRC made a final enforcement decision.

In response to the NOV, the Army committed to take a number of actions to correct the violation and prevent recurrence. These actions include, in part, (1) submitting a license application, and (2) ensuring that appropriate access control of areas suspected of containing DU is maintained to protect workers and members of the public.

Because the Army identified the issue and took or planned to take adequate corrective actions in a timely manner, the NRC did not propose a civil penalty, in accordance with the enforcement policy.

Violations Associated with Red and Yellow Findings

In CY 2011, the NRC issued NOVs associated with a red SDP finding to one reactor licensee and a yellow SDP finding to another reactor licensee. The NRC issued no violations associated with a red SDP finding and four violations associated with yellow findings issued in CY 2010. Short summaries of the cases issued in CY 2011 follow:

- On May 9, 2011, an NOV was issued to the Tennessee Valley Authority (TVA) for a violation associated with a red SDP finding identified in an inspection at the Browns Ferry Nuclear Power Plant. The violation involved the failure to implement an inservice testing program in accordance with the American Society of Mechanical Engineers (ASME) Code for Operation and Maintenance of Nuclear Power Plants (OM Code), 1995 Edition, 1996 Addenda, Section ISTC 4.1. In a letter dated June 8, 2011, TVA appealed the final significance determination of this red finding. The NRC performed an independent review of this finding and in a letter dated August 16, 2011, concluded that TVA failed to establish adequate programs, as required by 10 CFR 50.55a(b)3(ii), to ensure that motor-operated valves continued to be capable of performing their design-basis safety functions. The inadequacy of TVA's programs resulted in the Unit 1 Low Pressure Coolant Injection (LPCI) outboard injection valve, 1-FCV-74-66, being left in a significantly degraded condition and the Unit 1 LPCI/RHR Loop II unable to fulfill its safety function. The basis and outcome of the final risk significance determination evaluation on this red finding remained unchanged. As a result of this enforcement action, the NRC conducted additional inspection activities. On January 23, 2012, an NOV was issued to TVA for a SLIII violation of 10 CFR 50.9, "Completeness and Accuracy of Information" associated with this issue. Specifically, TVA gave information to the Commission that was not complete and accurate in all material respects, about its NRC Generic Letter 89-10, "Safety-Related Motor-Operator Valve Testing and Surveillance" testing program. Because the violation had occurred more than five years previously, the statute of limitation provisions in Title 28 to the United States Code, Section 2462, "Time for Commencing Proceedings," had tolled and no civil penalty could be assessed for this violation.

- On December 6, 2011, an NOV was issued to Duke Energy Carolinas, LLC (Licensee) for a violation associated with a yellow SDP finding identified in an inspection at the Oconee Nuclear Station. The Licensee identified that the installed pressurizer heater breakers supplying power from the standby shutdown facility (SSF) may not be able to withstand the expected containment temperatures during certain casualty scenarios and declared the system inoperable. Later the Licensee replaced these breakers and declared the system operable. However, the licensee performed limited environmental testing performed on these breakers and during subsequent environmental qualification testing it discovered that these new breakers could not perform their design-basis function at the expected elevated containment temperatures, so the Licensee declared them inoperable. The system was later declared operable when the Licensee replaced these breakers with environmentally qualified fuses. An NOV was included with the finding for a violation of 10 CFR Part 50, Appendix B, "Quality Assurance Criteria for Nuclear Power Plants," Criterion III, "Design Control." From 1983 to June 1, 2011, the Licensee implemented a modification to the SSF that used installed breakers that had not been tested to verify that they would function at elevated containment temperatures and maintain SSF functionality in accordance with the licensing and design basis.

B.   Hearing Activities

In CY 2011, a request was made for a hearing before the ASLB relating to enforcement actions against Mattingly Testing Services, Inc. (MTS or the Licensee) and its former president and owner. Although the ASLB established a review board, the case was successfully closed before the conduct of any adjudicatory proceeding when the board approved a settlement agreement that the NRC reached with the affected parties.

Mattingly Testing Services, Inc.

On September 2, 2010, an Immediately Effective Order Revoking License was issued to MTS for multiple violations that the NRC identified during an NRC inspection and investigation. On the same day, the NRC issued an Immediately Effective Order Prohibiting Involvement in NRC-Licensed Activities for a period of seven years to Mr. Mark Ficek, president and owner of MTS. Mr. Ficek did not agree with NRC's characterization of the issues and on September 22, 2010 requested, in accordance with the Order and 10 CFR 2.205, "Civil Penalties," that the ASLB conduct a hearing into these matters.

On October 6, 2010, the ASLB granted Mr. Ficek's request for a hearing to resolve issues associated with the two Orders the NRC issued on September 2, 2010. On the same date, the ASLB denied a request by Ms. Dayna Thompson, an employee of MTS, to forgo the immediate effectiveness of the MTS Order. On November 4, 2010, the Licensee and the NRC jointly submitted a motion asking the board to hold this administrative enforcement proceeding in abeyance, pending the outcome of proposed settlement negotiations.

On February 22, 2011, the ASLB approved a settlement agreement successfully negotiated between the NRC and Mr. Ficek. The board found that its terms reflected a fair and reasonable settlement of these matters in keeping with the objectives of the NRC's Enforcement Policy, and that they satisfied the requirements of 10 CFR 2.338(g) and 10 CFR 2.338(h). The ASLB Order approving and incorporating the settlement agreement superseded the September 2, 2010, Enforcement Orders to MTS and Mr. Ficek. The board's Order stipulates, in part, that Mr. Ficek will not own a controlling share or interest of an NRC licensee, Mr. Ficek will refrain from engaging in NRC-licensed activities until September 2, 2017, the revoked MTS license will not be reinstated, and for a period of three years, Mr. Ficek will give notice to the OE Director 10 days before beginning employment involving certain specified NRC-licensed activities. The complete Order can be viewed in ADAMS at Accession No. ML110530327. This action required extensive interaction and cooperation between Region IV, OE, OI, the Office of the General Counsel (OGC), and the Office of Federal and State Materials and Environmental Management (FSME) within the NRC and with the Federal Bureau of Investigation and the State of Wyoming.

C.   Orders

In CY 2011, the NRC issued 10 orders to licensees and to individuals. These included seven confirmatory orders that were issued to confirm commitments associated with ADR settlement agreements. Five of these orders included a requirement to pay a civil penalty as a result of the settlement agreements. One order was issued to a materials licensee suspending its licensed activities for failing to provide financial assurance for decommissioning.

Two of the orders were issued to individuals. One individual is prohibited from involvement in NRC-licensed activities until specific actions are taken to ensure reasonable assurance is provided for the protection of public health and safety. Another individual, who is no longer employed in NRC-licensed related activities, must notify the NRC of future involvement in NRC-licensed or Agreement State regulated activities.

As shown in Table 1, the number of orders the NRC issued in CY 2011 decreased from CY 2010 partly because of a decrease in the number of cases involving ADR and a decrease in the number of cases involving individuals.

Appendix C includes a brief description of the enforcement orders issued in CY 2011.

D.   Enforcement Actions Supported by the Office of Investigations

In CY 2011, an OI investigation supported 21 percent of the escalated enforcement actions (20 of the 96). This figure is consistent with the percentage supported by OI investigations in CY 2010. The escalated actions supported by OI investigations include the following:

- 9 of the 14 escalated NOVs with civil penalties (64 percent)
- 7 of the 77 escalated NOVs without civil penalties (9 percent)
- 9 of the 10 enforcement orders (90 percent)

The 21 enforcement actions supported by OI investigations are comparable to the 27 enforcement actions supported in CY 2010 and are a decrease in the average number of OI supported cases over previous years. The number of enforcement actions supported by an OI investigation also decreased from the 45 cases in CY 2009.

E.   Actions Involving Individuals and Nonlicensee Organizations

In CY 2011, the agency issued seven escalated enforcement actions to licensed and unlicensed individuals. This number is included in the total number of escalated enforcement actions (NOVs and orders) that the agency issued in CY 2011. Appendix C summarizes the orders that were issued to individuals and Appendix D summarizes the NOVs issued to individuals in CY 2011. These appendices do not include individual enforcement actions involving security related violations. The number of escalated actions issued to individuals in CY 2011 decreased from 11 escalated actions issued to individuals in CY 2010 and 17 issued in CY 2009.

The agency issued one escalated enforcement action to a nonlicensee organization in CY 2011. Appendix E summarizes this action.

F.   Enforcement Action Involving Discrimination

In CY 2011, one case involving an allegation of discrimination was resolved using post-investigation ADR. This is equivalent the number processed in CY 2010. On August 22, 2011, the NRC issued a confirmatory order (EA-11-096) to confirm commitments made as result of an ADR mediation session held on July 18, 2011, between Entergy Corporation and the NRC. This confirmatory order arose out of an apparent violation of 10 CFR 50.7, "Employee Protection," in which the NRC had reached a preliminary conclusion that an employee at the River Bend Station was rated lower in the 2008 annual performance appraisal, in part because the employee questioned the qualifications necessary to perform certain work activities in compliance with applicable plant procedures.

G.   Use of Judgment and Discretion in Determining Appropriate Enforcement Sanctions

The NRC may choose to exercise discretion and either escalate or mitigate enforcement sanctions or otherwise refrain from taking enforcement action within its statutory authority. The exercise of discretion allows the NRC to determine which actions should be taken in a particular case, notwithstanding the guidance contained in the Enforcement Policy. After considering the general tenets of the Enforcement Policy and the safety and security significance of a violation and its surrounding circumstances, the NRC may exercise judgment and discretion in determining the severity levels of violations and the appropriate enforcement sanctions.

In CY 2011, the NRC exercised enforcement discretion in 34 cases to address violations of NRC requirements, the same number as CY 2010. Below is a discussion of the more significant cases dispositioned with discretion in CY 2011.

1.   Discretion Involving Enforcement Guidance

In 22 cases the NRC used discretion in accordance with either the Interim Enforcement Policy guidance related to fire protection issues or Enforcement Guidance Memoranda (EGM).

- The NRC continued to perform fire protection inspections at power reactor sites to verify compliance with requirements of 10 CFR 50, Appendix R, "Fire Protection Program for Nuclear Power Facilities Operating Prior to January 1, 1979." Violations of these requirements that were identified at sites transitioning to the National Fire Protection Association Standard 805 (NFPA 805) and met the criteria as stated in the Interim Enforcement Policy, "Enforcement Discretion for Certain Fire Protection Issues (10 CFR 50.48)" warranted enforcement discretion and notices of violation were not issued. Five documented cases involved this type of discretion. Violations that involved multiple fire-induced circuit faults identified at sites that are not transitioning to NFPA 805 and that meet the criteria as stated in the Enforcement Guidance Memoranda (EGM)-09-002, "Enforcement Discretion For Certain Fire Induced Circuit Faults", also warranted enforcement discretion. Two documented case involved this type of discretion.

- The agency dispositioned nine violations using discretion in accordance with EGM-09-004, "Interim Guidance for Dispositioning Violations of Naturally Occurring and Accelerator-Produced Radioactive Materials (NARM) Requirements," dated May 13, 2009. Enforcement discretion may be exercised for violations of the NARM requirements if certain criteria are met as described in EGM-09-004.

- The NRC dispositioned five violations using discretion in accordance with EGM-11-004, "Interim Guidance for Dispositioning Violations of Security Requirements for Portable Gauges," dated April 28, 2011. Enforcement discretion may be exercised for violations of 10 CFR 30.34(i) if certain criteria are met as described in EGM-11-004.

- The NRC dispositioned one violation using discretion in accordance with EGM-09-007, Revision 2, "Interim Guidance for Dispositionng Violations of National Source Tracking System (NSTS) Requirements," dated March 2, 2011. Enforcement discretion may be exercised for violations of NSTS requirements if certain criteria are met as described in EGM-09-007, Revision 2.

2.   Discretion Involving Special Circumstances

Eleven cases involved use of discretion in accordance with Section 3.5 of the Enforcement Policy, "Special Circumstances." In each case, the staff determined that the facts supported issuance of a closeout letter to the licensee in lieu of an NOV. Below is a discussion of the more significant cases dispositioned in CY 2011.

- A violation of 10 CFR 20.1301(a)(1), normally categorized at SL III, was dispositioned using enforcement discretion in accordance with Section 3.5 of the Enforcement Policy. Because of a malfunctioning fixed nuclear gauge at a materials licensee, six individuals received radiation exposures in excess of regulatory limits for non-radiation workers, which is 0.1 rem. The NRC determined that the gauge was defective and concluded that the equipment failure could not have been avoided or detected by the licensee. The licensee responded appropriately when aware of the defect to prevent additional unintended personnel radiation exposures. In recognition of the corrective actions taken by the licensee and the circumstances surrounding the event, the NRC refrained from issuing any violation in this case.

- The NRC dispositioned violations involving small reactor coolant system leakage at four operating reactors in accordance with Section 3.5 of the Enforcement Policy. In each case, the staff concluded that although any reactor coolant system leakage at power constitutes a violation, the licensee's actions did not contribute to a degraded condition, and were reasonable to identify and address the matter.

- Violations of 10 CFR 50, Appendix B, Criterion III, "Design Control," normally categorized at SL IV, were dispositioned at four reactor facilities in accordance with Section 3.5 of the Enforcement Policy. In two cases, the licensees failed to ensure that the power supplies for steam generator power operated relief valves met the design bases. The NRC concluded that because a compliance backfit was issued to resolve the technical issue, the violation resulted from matters not reasonably within the licensee's ability to foresee and correct. The other two cases involved (1) failure to protect safety-related equipment from flooding, and (2) failure to ensure adequate electrical separation between a safety-related and a nonsafety related system. In both of these cases, the NRC concluded that the violation resulted from matters not reasonably within the licensee's ability to foresee and correct.

3.   Discretion Used to Forego Proposing a Civil Penalty

The staff exercised enforcement discretion, in accordance with Section 3.6 of the Enforcement Policy, to forego proposing a civil penalty in one case to ensure that the enforcement action properly reflected the significance of the circumstances of the violation. This enforcement action differed from the action that would have resulted from application of the normal civil penalty assessment process described in Section 2.3.4 of the Enforcement Policy. In CY 2010, the staff exercised enforcement discretion to forego proposing a civil penalty in one case and exercised enforcement discretion in another case to escalate the amount of a proposed civil penalty.

- The NRC concluded that enforcement discretion to forego proposing a civil penalty was appropriate in the case of an Alaska Industrial X-Ray SLIII violation involving a security issue identified in an NRC letter dated June 7, 2011. The basis for the agency's conclusion was that the licensee had significantly improved its compliance with NRC requirements since the last enforcement action and timeliness factors associated with plant security systems. Normally, a base civil penalty in the amount of $7,000 would be proposed for a violation of this type. Further details are not provided because of the security nature of the violation.

4.   Notices of Enforcement Discretion

Occasionally, circumstances may arise in which a power reactor licensee's compliance with a technical specification or other license condition would require a plant transient or performance testing, inspection, or other system realignment that is of greater risk than the current specific plant conditions. In these circumstances, the NRC staff may choose not to enforce the applicable requirements. The staff exercises this enforcement discretion, designated as a notice of enforcement discretion (NOED) in accordance with Section 3.7 of the Enforcement Policy, only if it is clearly satisfied that the action is consistent with protecting the public health and safety. The staff may also issue NOEDs in cases involving severe weather or other natural phenomena when it determines that exercising this discretion will not compromise safety. NOEDs require justification from a licensee or certificate holder that documents the safety basis for the request and provides whatever other information the staff deems necessary to issue an NOED. The NRC issued two NOEDs in CY 2011.

- NOED 11-4-001, verbally granted enforcement discretion on August 14, 2011, to Wolf Creek Nuclear Operating Corporation (Wolf Creek Generating Station), that allowed the license to extend the 72-hour completion time for Technical Specification 3.7.5, "Auxiliary Feedwater System," Required Actions C.1 and C.2, by 24-hours to restore the turbine driven auxiliary feedwater (TDAFW) pump to an operable status or commence a plant shutdown. The licensee commenced a shutdown of the unit approximately one hour before the expiration of the NOED and returned the unit to full power when the TDAFW pump was declared operable approximately one hour after the NOED expired.

- NOED 11-3-001, verbally granted enforcement discretion on September 29, 2011, to Northern States Power Company (Monticello Nuclear Generating Plant), that allowed the licensee to extend the 12-hour completion time for Technical Specification 3.8.1, "AC Sources – Operating," Required Action F.1., by 5 days to restore a diesel generator to operable status or commence a plant shutdown. On October 3, 2011, the 11 emergency diesel generator was declared operable following successful testing.

NOEDs issued to power reactor licensees and gaseous diffusion plants can be found on the NRC's Web site at http://www.nrc.gov/reading-rm/doc-collections/enforcement/notices/.

H.   Withdrawn Actions

Licensees can challenge enforcement actions for several reasons; for example, a licensee might dispute the requirements, the facts of the case, the agency's application of the Enforcement Policy, or the significance of the violation. Licensees may provide clarifying information that was not available at the time of the inspection, and this may affect a finding of noncompliance.

In addition, OE has established a metric for quality of enforcement actions based on the number of disputed and withdrawn nonescalated enforcement actions. The goal is less than 30 withdrawn nonescalated enforcement actions in a calendar year. This metric does not include violations that are withdrawn on the basis of supplemental information that was not available to an inspector before the assessment of an enforcement sanction. In CY 2011, the agency issued approximately 1,200 nonescalated enforcement actions to reactor, materials, and fuel facility licensees. This is an increase of approximately 20 percent over the number of nonescalated enforcement actions issued annually in the past two years. Of these actions, 10 nonescalated enforcement actions were disputed. This is a slight decrease from the 12 nonescalated enforcement actions disputed in CY 2010. In CY 2011, the NRC withdrew four of these disputed actions. This is an increase from the one nonescalated enforcement action withdrawn in CY 2010.

In CY 2011, the agency issued 96 escalated enforcement actions to reactors, materials, and fuel facility licensees, of which none were disputed. In CY 2010, two escalated enforcement actions were disputed and both were withdrawn.

III. Ongoing Activities

A. Enforcement Policy

The NRC Enforcement Policy is a living document that is periodically revised to reflect regulatory changes, experience, and stakeholder input. On August 27, 2010, the Commission approved the latest revision to the Enforcement Policy (Staff Requirements Memorandum (SRM) -SECY-09-0190). This SRM also directed the NRC staff to evaluate specific topics for inclusion in a future policy revision. Those topics included guidance for (1) determining when daily civil penalties are appropriate; (2) providing credit to fuel cycle licensees with effective corrective action programs; and (3) reevaluating the Enforcement Policy related to construction activities, including cases for which discretion may be appropriate.

This latest revised Policy became effective on September 30, 2010 (75 FR 60485). Some of the significant changes in the 2010 Policy included: (1) increasing from eight to 14 the violation example activity areas; (2) adding base civil penalties for uranium enrichment facilities and high level waste repositories; (3) increasing the base civil penalty for uranium conversion facilities; and (4) adding a glossary of enforcement terms.

1. Interim Enforcement Policy Guidance

In CY 2011, the staff developed two Interim Enforcement Policy guidance documents that were incorporated into the existing Enforcement Policy available (ADAMS Accession No. ML093480037).

- In March of 2008, the NRC updated the requirements in 10 CFR Part 26, "Fitness for Duty Programs," by reorganizing the rule and adding Subpart I, "Managing Fatigue." Subsequently, between 2009 and 2010, the NRC received several petitions from outside stakeholders for rulemaking related to the new rule, along with a request for enforcement discretion on the minimum days off (MDO) provision of the rule. The staff evaluated the petitions and determined that an alternative to the MDO requirement of the new rule was needed until the rule could be amended. As a result, the staff developed guidance to grant enforcement discretion for violations of the MDO requirement if certain criteria are met and incorporated this relief through the issuance of an Interim Enforcement Policy, "Enforcement Discretion for the Minimum Days Off Requirements of § 26.205(d)(3). The Interim Enforcement Policy became effective on April 25, 2011. On July 21, 2011, the NRC issued the final rule amending 10 CFR Part 26, including the alternative to the MDO requirement. At that time, the Interim Enforcement Policy regarding the MDO requirement expired.

- Because of the unforeseen complexity involved in the transition process to National Fire Protection Association Standard 805 (NFPA 805), the Interim Enforcement Policy, "Enforcement Discretion for Certain Fire Protection Issues (10 CFR 50.48)" has undergone a number of revisions that have changed the license amendment request (LAR) submittal due date for many licensees. This change in submittal dates created a "grouping effect," and the NRC expected to receive approximately 23 LARs by the end of June 2011. The Commission approved a staggered submittal schedule that was necessary to ensure timely review of these and other LARs. On July 12, 2011, the staff issued Interim Enforcement Policy that granted enforcement discretion to incorporate this new submittal schedule.

2.   Future Enforcement Policy Revision Activities

In CY 2011, the staff focused on activities related to the Commission's directives for further revisions to the Enforcement Policy.

- On March 21, 2011, SRM – SECY-10-0140, "Options for Revising the Construction Reactor Oversight Process Assessment Program," (Adams Accession No. ML110800557) directed the staff to develop a construction assessment program for nuclear power plants that includes (1) a regulatory framework; (2) the use of a construction significance determination process to determine the significance of findings identified during the construction inspection program; and, (3) the use of a construction action matrix to determine the appropriate NRC response to findings.

- On August 9, 2011, a *Federal Register* Notice (76 FR 48919) announced that the NRC was reevaluating construction-related topics in the Enforcement Policy and was soliciting comments on revisions recommended by the staff. The proposed changes would clarify sections that had not explicitly included construction activities, revise how the NRC dispositions NCVs and clarify and revise how the NRC expects to exercise enforcement discretion at construction sites.

- On August 30, 2011, the NRC conducted a public meeting to discuss the proposed changes to the Construction Policy.

- On September 6, 2011, the NRC published a *Federal Register* Notice (76 FR 54986) announcing that it was proposing several changes to the Enforcement Policy to address additional items in SRM-SECY-09-0190 and additional changes proposed by the staff.

- On November 1, 2011, OE issued SECY-11-0155, "Proposed Changes to the Enforcement Policy Associated with Construction Activities." Proposed changes to the Policy included, but were not limited to, changes to clarify the current Policy, revisions to Section 2.3.2, "Noncited Violation," and revisions to Policy sections on Enforcement discretion.

- On December 6, 2011, the NRC published a *Federal Register* Notice (76 FR 76192) requesting comments from the public and other stakeholders on the additional proposed changes to the Policy. This notice also solicited comments on the effectiveness of the September 30, 2010, revision of the Policy, which the staff committed to do in SECY-09-0190.

- On January 24, 2012, the NRC Office of International Programs and OE held a public meeting, in part to provide an opportunity for the Nuclear Energy Institute, industry representatives, and the public to discuss changes to the Policy related to the export and import of nuclear equipment and material.

B. Enforcement Guidance Memoranda

OE issues EGMs to provide guidance on the interpretation of specific provisions of the Enforcement Policy. A link to the full text of all publicly available EGMs appears in Appendix A to the NRC Enforcement Manual. The office issued seven EGMs in CY 2011 summarized below.

- March 2, 2011, EGM-09-007 (rev 2), "Interim Guidance for Dispositioning Violations of National Source Tracking System (NSTS) Requirements". The purpose of this EGM is to provide guidance for the disposition of inspection findings related to a licensee's implementation of national source tracking system requirements.

- April 28, 2011, EGM 11-004, "Interim Guidance for Dispositioning Violations of Security Requirements for Portable Gauges". The purpose of this EGM is to provide guidance for the disposition of violations involving the failure to maintain the required minimum of two independent physical controls to include a provision for enforcement discretion for certain violations related to the security requirements for portable gauges.

- June 3, 2011, EGM 11-002, "Enforcement Discretion for Licensee-Identified Violations at Power Reactor Construction Sites Pursuant to 10 CFR Part 52". The purpose of this EGM is to clarify the guidance for exercising enforcement discretion in dispositioning SL IV licensee-identified violations at power reactors that are under construction as NCVs.

- August 31, 2011, EGM 11-001, "Pilot Program for Modified Enforcement Panel Process". The purpose of this EGM is to provide guidance for implementing a modified enforcement panel pilot program for enforcement cases that meet certain criteria and to improve efficiency, timeliness, and effectiveness.

- October 4, 2011, EGM 11-003, "Dispositioning Boiling Water Reactor Licensee Non-Compliance with Technical Specification Containment Requirements During Operations with a Potential for Draining the Reactor Vessel". The purpose of this EGM is to provide guidance on how to disposition boiling water reactor licensee noncompliance with technical specification containment requirements during operations with a potential for draining the reactor vessel (OPDRV).

- December 5, 2011, EGM 11-005, "Post-Investigation Alternative Dispute Resolution Program". The purpose of this EGM is to offer guidance for agreements reached between parties engaged in the NRC's post-investigation alternative dispute (ADR) program.

- December 21, 2011, EGM 11-006, "Enforcement Actions Related to the Construction Reactor Oversight Process". The purpose of this EGM is to provide guidance for dispositioning enforcement actions during the Construction Reactor Oversight Process (cROP) pilot program. A 1 year pilot program for the draft process discussed in SRM-SECY-10-0140, "Options for Revising the Construction Reactor Oversight Process Assessment Program," began on January 1, 2012. The staff recognized that additional Enforcement Policy changes related to construction may be required on the basis of experience gained during this pilot and issued this EGM.

C. Knowledge Management

In CY 2011, OE engaged in several knowledge-management activities. Some of the ongoing activities being conducted to maintain an adequate knowledge base included supporting training, completing reviews and self assessments, developing internal office procedures, and conducting counterpart meetings.

Enforcement Counterpart Meetings

In May 2011, regional and Headquarters enforcement staff held a counterpart meeting to discuss ways to improve the enforcement process and communications among staff. The meeting resulted in a number of action items to improve the enforcement program. Examples included: (1) coordinate with OGC to obtain more definitive guidance regarding licensee accountability as it relates to the offsite activities of an individual (specifically, the failure to report arrest); (2) ensure the proposed revision to Management Directive 3.5 specifies that ADR sessions are to be publicly noticed; (3) develop SLIV example for Emergency Action Level (EAL); (4) develop a nonpublic system for capturing OGC interpretations; (5) revise the Prohibition Order boilerplate to reflect the agency's views; and (6) support discussions about the severity level structure of medical event reporting violations. In addition, a working group was established to develop recommendations to improve efficiency of the enforcement panel process. Improvement of this specific area was an ongoing effort during the year.

Training

OE supported members of the Leadership Potential Program and the Nuclear Safety Professional Development Program on rotational assignments to the office. The knowledge gained by those staff members will improve understanding of the Enforcement Program in the field. In addition, OE staff members participated in rotational assignments in other offices (FSME, the Office of Nuclear Reactor Regulation (NRR), and the Office of Nuclear Materials Safety and Safeguards (NMSS)) and Region IV. OE staff supported the regions in a number of ways. Examples include (1) participating in the minor/greater than minor working group for the construction inspection program; and (2) acting as a regional enforcement specialist for an extended period of time in two separate regions.

Headquarters and regional enforcement staff engaged in outreach opportunities to internal stakeholders on enforcement and ADR processes during counterpart meetings and other office training sessions. Examples included multiple training sessions provided by OE gave on the revised Enforcement Policy.

Reviews and Self Assessments

The OE Operating Plan requires that OE staff annually conduct specific topic focused assessments of the materials and reactor enforcement programs to assess consistent application of the Enforcement Policy. In CY 2011, OE completed self-assessments of (1) the use of 591 forms for dispositioning nonescalated violations by materials licensees; and, (2) the 3-week e-mail process for the disposition of unsubstantiated allegations. These assessments developed a number of recommended improvement items but generally found the enforcement process was being effectively implemented

In CY 2011, OE completed two Regional Enforcement Assessments conducted in accordance with Office Instruction ADM-110, "Conduct of Enforcement Program Assessments." In February 2011, an assessment was completed in Region III and in August 2011, an assessment was completed in Region IV. Each assessment was performed by a team of enforcement specialists from OE and one of the other regions. The primary purpose of these assessments was to ensure that the enforcement program is being consistently implemented in the region. The assessments also provided the opportunity to share "best practices" between the regions and to enhance knowledge management of the enforcement process. The assessments involved the review of nonescalated enforcement actions and processes, which do not normally involve Headquarters. The teams concluded that both Region III and Region IV maintain strong regional enforcement programs and are effectively implementing the NRC Enforcement Policy largely because of the efficient and effective collaboration among inspectors, enforcement and allegation coordination staff, and regional and division management.

D.   Regional Accomplishments

In CY 2011, the regions conducted both routine and focused self assessments of the enforcement area to ensure effective performance and to identify opportunities for continuous improvement. The self-assessments encompassed both the reactor and materials arenas; considered performance associated with development and issuance of both nonescalated and escalated enforcement actions; and included activities that required a high degree of coordination with other NRC stakeholders, such as OI.

These assessments included the following reviews:

- new reactor and fuel facility construction inspection reports related to nonescalated enforcement actions
- nonescalated enforcement actions containing safeguards information
- the inadvertent distribution of an individual closeout letter not intended for public release
- management of low-level wrongdoing issues that resulted in NCVs
- comparison of regional instructions compared to guidance in the Enforcement Policy, Enforcement Manual, management directives, and inspection procedures

Overall, the self-assessments showed that the regions were effectively implementing the Enforcement Program. Recommendations were made for expediting the investigation, evaluation, and issuance of enforcement actions issues of low-level wrongdoing.

In addition to assessments, the enforcement staff trained regional technical staff, in part, on the revised Enforcement Policy, recent EGMs, and proper enforcement documentation requirements for inspectors and participated on inspector qualification review boards as necessary.

Regional enforcement representatives supported agency enforcement initiatives and activities including the following:

- the Lean Six Sigma Post-Investigation project
- the intermediate timeliness goal improvement project
- escalated enforcement working group

Table 3: CY 2011—Escalated Enforcement Actions by Region and Program Office

Program Office	Escalated NOVs (w/o Civil Penalty)	Civil Penalties[1]	Orders[2]	Orders Imposing Civil Penalty	TOTAL
Region I	22	4	1	0	27
Region II	10	3	1	0	14
Region III	23	1	2	0	26
Region IV	18	6	0	0	24
FSME	1	0	0	0	1
NMSS	1	0	0	0	1
NSIR	2	0	0	0	2
OE	0	0	1	0	1
TOTAL	**77**	**14**	**5**	**0**	**96**

---

[1] Includes Orders with Civil Penalties (1 for Region I; 1 for Region III; 3 for Region IV)
[2] Does not include 5 Orders with Civil Penalties

Table 4: CY 2011—Escalated Enforcement Actions by Type of Licensee, Nonlicensee, or Individual

Type of Licensee	Escalated NOVs (w/o Civil Penalty)	Civil Penalty[1]	Orders[2]	Orders Imposing Civil Penalty	TOTAL
Operating Reactor	27	0	1	0	28
Gauge User	13	2	0	0	15
Hospital	13	1	0	0	14
Radiographer	8	3	0	0	11
Fuel Facility	3	3	1	0	7
Irradiator	3	0	0	0	3
Materials Distributor	1	1	1	0	3
Unlicensed Individual (Materials)	1	0	1	0	2
Unlicensed Individual (Reactor)	2	0	0	0	2
Well Logger	0	2	0	0	2
Unlicensed Individual (Fuel Facility)	1	0	0	0	1
Licensed Individual (Reactor)	1	0	0	0	1
Nonlicensee	1	0	0	0	1
Physician	0	0	1	0	1
Pharmacy	0	0	0	0	0
Academic	0	0	0	0	0
UF Conversion Facility	0	0	0	0	0
Research Reactor	0	0	0	0	0
Mill	0	0	0	0	0
Radiographer Fabricator	0	0	0	0	0
Waste Disposal	0	0	0	0	0
Other	3	3	0	0	6
TOTAL	77	14	5	0	96

[1] Includes Orders with Civil Penalties (1 for Well Logger; 1 for Hospital; 3 for Radiographer)
[2] Does not include 5 Orders with Civil Penalties

Appendix A: Summary of Cases Involving Civil Penalties[*]

Civil Penalties Issued To Reactor Licensees

NONE

Civil Penalties Involving Confirmatory Orders Issued To Material Licensees

Accurate NDE and Inspection, LC   EA-11-043
Broussard, LA

On December 19, 2011, an Immediately Effective Confirmatory Order was issued to
Accurate NDE and Inspection, LLC (Accurate), to confirm commitments made as a result of
an Alternative Dispute Resolution (ADR) mediation session held on September 28, 2011.
This enforcement action is based on two willful violations involving (1) the failure to maintain
accurate personnel monitoring information; and (2) the failure to comply with a state license
requirement for radiographers to notify the licensee radiation safety officer (RSO) before
attempting to retrieve a disconnected source. Three additional violations were identified
involving (1) the failure to wear personnel dosimeters while performing radiographic
operations; (2) the failure to conduct a radiation survey when a radiographic exposure
device was placed into storage; and (3) the failure to immediately report the loss of a sealed
source. Accurate agreed to take a number of actions including (1) providing and recording
initial and annual training to deter willful violations and address specified related topics; (2)
developing and submitting procedures for training the RSO or any manager designated to
be on-call; (3) submitting copies of procedures to the NRC when performing radiographic
operations in NRC jurisdiction; and (4) paying a civil penalty in the amount of $13,500.

Alaska Industrial X-Ray, Inc.   EA-10-231
Anchorage, AK

On June 7, 2011, an Immediately Effective Confirmatory Order was issued to Alaska
Industrial X-Ray Inc. (AIX) to confirm commitments made as a result of an Alternative
Dispute Resolution (ADR) mediation session held on April 19, 2011. This enforcement
action is based on a deliberate violation associated with two conditions of the Order
Modifying License (EA-08-196): (1) failure to have an independent consultant or contractor
perform field audits and submit the audit reports to AIX and the NRC, as required by
Condition 1 of the Order, from August 2008 through March 2010 and (2) failure to have an
independent consultant or a contractor evaluate the effectiveness of AIX's radiation safety
program, as required by Condition 3 of the Order, from September 2008 through October
2010. AIX agreed to take a number of actions including (1) training all AIX employees
engaged in licensed activities on what is meant by willfulness; (2) conducting an annual
review of its radiation safety and compliance program by an independent auditor; (3)
conducting quarterly audits of AIX radiographers as they perform radiography; and (4)
paying a civil penalty in the amount of $1,000.

---

[*] *Please note that cases involving security-related issues are not included*

Bozeman Deaconess Hospital   EA-10-258
Bozeman, MT

On July 8, 2011, an Immediately Effective Confirmatory Order was issued to Bozeman Deaconess Hospital (BDH) to confirm commitments made as a result of an ADR mediation session held on May 25, 2011. This enforcement action is based on two willful violations involving (1) the failure to secure licensed materials from unauthorized removal or access as required by 10 CFR 20.1801; and (2) the failure to control and maintain constant surveillance of licensed material as required by 10 CFR 20.1802. BDH agreed to take a number of actions including (1) providing training to hospital staff and managers involved in NRC licensed activities by an independent third-party organization; (2) modifying the internal requirements for new worker training for its annual refresher training; (3) developing and implementing a procedure that allows hospital employees and contractors to raise radiation safety concerns to hospital management; and (4) paying a civil penalty in the amount of $3,500.

Professional Service Industries, Inc.   EA-10-161
Oakbrook Terrace, IL

On August 18, 2011, an Immediately Effective Confirmatory Order was issued to Professional Service Industries, Inc. (PSI), to confirm commitments made as a result of an ADR mediation session held on July 11, 2011. This enforcement action is based on eight violations as well as security-related violations involving the performance of industrial radiography in the Rock Springs, Wyoming area. In addition, the NRC indicated that willfulness on the part of an office manager and a radiographer appeared to have been a factor in two of the violations. PSI made no admission that they deliberately violated any NRC requirement. PSI agreed to take a number of actions including (1) developing and implementing a disciplinary program managed by the corporate staff that provides a graded approach for radiation safety and security infractions; (2) enhanced routine and refresher training for staff; (3) annual safety culture training for Radiation Safety Officers; (4) enhanced annual audits of the Radiation Safety Program; (5) advance notification if PSI will be working in NRC jurisdiction under reciprocity; and (6) paying a civil penalty in the amount of $15,000. Prior to issuance of this enforcement action PSI voluntarily terminated its NRC license for radiography but maintains Agreement State licenses for radiography and an NRC license for other non-radiographic, regulated activities.

Superior Well Services, ltd.   EA-10-077
Indiana, PA

On February 8, 2011, an Immediately Effective Confirmatory Order was issued to the Superior Well Services, Ltd. (SWS) to confirm commitments made as a result of an ADR mediation session held on January 4, 2011. The licensee requested ADR following the NRC's October 21, 2010 Notice of Violation and Proposed Civil Penalty in the amount of $34,000, involving five violations that were categorized into two severity level (SL) III problems. The first SL III problem involved three violations related to the temporary loss of two radioactive well logging sources. The second SL III problem involved two violations related to the deliberate failure to conduct radiological surveys and the creation of inaccurate survey records. SWS agreed to (1) take corrective actions addressing all of the violations; (2) ensure that the corrective actions are effective; and (3) ensure that lessons learned from these events are extended to the well logging industry. In addition, SWS took several corrective actions prior to the ADR mediation session. In recognition of SWS's proposed corrective actions, in addition to corrective actions already taken, the NRC agreed to reduce the civil penalty originally proposed to $17,000.

Civil Penalties Involving Notices of Violation Issued To Material Licensees

International Cyclotron, Inc.   EA-11-086
Hato Rey, PR

On December 19, 2011, a Notice of Violation and Proposed Imposition of a Civil Penalty in the amount of $7,000, and an Order suspending licensed activities within 60 days, was issued to International Cyclotron, Inc. (ICI), for a Severity Level III violation involving the failure to provide a decommissioning funding plan as required by 10 CFR 30.35. Specifically, on August 20, 2009, ICI was issued an NRC license authorizing the possession and use of unsealed byproduct material of applicable quantities set forth in Appendix B to 10 CFR Part 30 and ICI had not provided a decommissioning funding plan that contains a signed original of the financial instrument obtained to provide financial assurance for decommissioning, as required by 10 CFR 30.35. Further, based on ICI's failure to fully and timely respond to repeat NRC requests for information, and to compel ICI to comply with NRC regulations, the NRC issued an Order Suspending Licensed Activities (Order). According to this Order, if ICI does not submit to the NRC an acceptable financial assurance instrument within 60 days of the date of the Order, ICI is required to suspend all activities authorized under its License. This Order will remain in effect until ICI submits a financial assurance instrument and the NRC informs ICI that the instrument is accepted.

Luzenac America, Inc.   EA-11-022
Three Forks, MT

On July 7, 2011, a Notice of Violation and Proposed Imposition of Civil Penalty in the amount of $8,500 was issued to Luzenac America, Inc., for a Severity Level III violation involving the failure to transfer a device containing byproduct material to a licensee authorized to receive it, as required by 10 CFR 31.5(c)(8)(i). Specifically, as of December 2, 2010, Luzenac transferred a fixed nuclear gauge containing byproduct material to a recycling company that was not authorized to receive it.

Civil Penalties Issued To Fuel Cycle Licensees

Global Nuclear Fuel – Americas   EA-11-095
Wilmington, NC

On November 14, 2011, a Notice of Violation and Proposed Imposition of Civil Penalty in the amount of $17,500 was issued to Global Nuclear Fuel-Americas, LLC for a Severity Level III problem involving the failure to maintain the double contingency principle as it was compromised during the operation of the sinter test grinder and the risk of a high consequence event (criticality accident) increased. The NRC determined that five violations of NRC requirements directly related to the root causes that allowed the event occurred. Specifically, (1) on March 1, 2011, the licensee failed to ensure that a process design incorporated sufficient margins of safety to require at least two unlikely, independent, and concurrent changes in process conditions before a criticality accident was possible; (2) on March 1, 2011, the licensee failed to apply sufficient controls to the extent needed to reduce the likelihood of occurrence of a criticality, high-consequence event, in the sinter test grinder HEPA filter enclosure so that, upon implementation of such controls, the event was highly unlikely; (3) on February 4, 2009, the licensee failed to verify as part of the change process that the controls selected and installed for the sinter test grinder HEPA enclosure would limit the UO2 holdup to less than 25 kgs by controlling a differential pressure across the ventilation housing to 4-inches of water or less;   (4) on February 18, 2009, the licensee failed to conduct a criticality safety analysis (CSA) on the sinter test grinder; and (5) on August 1, 2010, and January 23, 2011, the licensee failed to notify HVAC and the area manager and request a clean out of the effected Sinter Test Grinder Primary HEPA Filter housing transition when the survey results for the transition exceeded the action limit of 0.5 mr/hr above background.

Orders Imposing a Civil Penalty

NONE

Appendix B: Summary of Escalated Notices of Violation Without Civil Penalties[*]

Notices Issued To Power Reactor Licensees

Carolina Power and Light Company   EA-11-251
Brunswick Steam Electric Plant

On December 27, 2011, an NOV was issued to Carolina Power and Light Company for a violation of 10 CFR 50, Appendix B, Criterion XVI, "Corrective Action" identified as a result of an inspection at the Brunswick Steam Electric Plant. The violation was associated with a White SDP finding involving the failure of personnel to promptly identify and correct a condition adverse to quality involving the external flood barrier for the emergency diesel generator fuel oil tank rooms as of April 20, 2011. Specifically, the entrance enclosures that house the emergency diesel generator fuel oil tanks had several openings, unsealed pinholes, and a narrow gap along the perimeter of the base walls, which would allow water intrusion into the emergency diesel generator fuel oil tank rooms during a design basis external event (hurricane).

Carolina Power and Light Company   EA-10-257
H. B. Robinson Steam Electric Plant

On January 31, 2011, an NOV was issued to Carolina Power and Light Company for two violations associated with two White SDP findings identified as a result of an inspection at the H. B. Robinson Steam Electric Plant. The first violation involved the failure to adequately implement multiple procedures during an uncontrolled cooldown of the Reactor Coolant System and subsequent safety injection as required by Technical Specifications 5.8.1, "Procedures." Specifically, on March 28, 2010, following a reactor trip, the licensee: (1) failed to take required procedural actions to stop an uncontrolled cooldown that resulted in a safety injection; (2) failed to identify a loss of component cooling water flow to the thermal barrier heat exchangers coincident with a failure to identify a loss of charging pump suction that resulted in inadequate seal injection flow; and (3) re-energized electrically faulted equipment that damaged surrounding equipment and resulted in electrical ground alarms, which required an Alert emergency declaration. The second violation involved failure to adequately design and implement operator training based on learning objectives as required by 10CFR55.59(c)4. Specifically, prior to March 28, 2010, training lesson material failed to identify the basis of a procedural action involving reactor coolant pump seal cooling required by a systems approach to training as defined in 10CFR55.4.

---

[*] *Please note that cases involving security-related issues are not included*

Dominion Nuclear Connecticut, Inc   EA-11-047
Millstone Power Station

On August 8, 2011, an NOV was issued to Dominion Nuclear Connecticut, Inc for two violations associated with a White SDP finding identified as a result of an inspection at the Millstone Power Station. The first violation involved the failure to implement procedures for safe operation and shutdown as required by Technical Specification 6.8, "Procedures." The second violation involved the failure to develop adequate procedures recommended in Regulatory Guide 1.33, February 1978, as required by Technical Specification 6.8. These failures caused and/or exacerbated an unanticipated eight percent reactor power increase at Unit 2 during main turbine control valve testing, which occurred on February 12, 2011.

Duke Energy Carolinas   EA-11-226
Oconee Nuclear Station

On December 6, 2011, an NOV was issued to Duke Energy Carolinas, LLC for a violation of 10 CFR 50, Appendix B, Criterion III, "Design Control" identified as a result of an inspection at the Oconee Nuclear Station. The violation was associated with a Yellow SDP finding involving the failure to perform a review for suitability of application of equipment essential to safety-related functions of structures, systems, and components. Specifically, Oconee personnel failed to maintain the Standby Shutdown Facility pressurizer heater breakers and associated electrical components in accordance with the licensing and design basis of the plant, which resulted in the Standby Shutdown Facility being inoperable from 1983, until June 1, 2011. (See Section II of this report for additional information).

Entergy Nuclear Operations   EA-11-174
Pilgrim Nuclear Power Station

On November 21, 2011, an NOV was issued to Entergy Nuclear Operations, Inc. for a violation of Technical Specification 5.4, "Procedures" identified as a result of an inspection at the Pilgrim Nuclear Power Station. The violation was associated with a White SDP finding involving multiple examples of failure to conduct safety-related activities as described in written procedures prior to and during a reactor startup operation. Specifically, on May 10, 2011, Pilgrim personnel failed to implement conduct of operations and reactivity control standards and procedures during a reactor startup which resulted in a reactor scram.

Exelon Generation Company, LLC   EA-11-014
Byron Station

On March 14, 2011, an NOV was issued to Exelon Generation Company, LLC for a violation of 10 CFR 50, Appendix B, Criterion V, "Instructions, Procedures, and Drawings" identified as a result of an inspection at the Byron Station. The violation was associated with a White SDP finding involving the failure to provide appropriate quantitative or qualitative acceptance criteria related to maintenance on the 2A emergency diesel generator. Specifically, on January 17, 2010, a work order package did not contain a final torque verification to ensure that the 2A diesel generator upper lube oil cooler spool piece connections were torqued to the required values. As a result, the spool piece flange connection to the upper lube oil cooler did not meet the minimum torque ranges, and, subsequently, during routine testing on November 17, 2010, the flange connection on the 2A diesel generator upper lube oil cooler failed. Because the 2A diesel generator was inoperable since January 17, 2010, and because the licensee was not aware of the inoperability, the Technical Specification allowed outage time of 14 days was also exceeded.

Exelon Generation Company   EA-11-221
Limerick Generating Station

On December 8, 2011, an NOV was issued to Exelon Generation Company, LLC for two violations associated with a White SDP finding identified as a result of an inspection at the Limerick Generating Station. The first violation involved the failure to establish adequate procedures as of April 23, 2011, for securing feedwater long-path flushing as required by Technical Specification 6.8, "Procedures." The second violation involved operating in Modes 1, 2, and 3 between April 23, 2011 and May 23, 2011, when a Primary Containment Isolation Valve and the Reactor Core Isolation Cooling System were inoperable, contrary to the requirements of Technical Specification 3.6.3, "Primary Containment Isolation Valves."

First Energy Nuclear Operating Company   EA-11-148
Perry Nuclear Power Plant

On August 25, 2011, an NOV was issued to First Energy Nuclear Operating Company for three violations associated with a White SDP finding identified as a result of an inspection at the Perry Nuclear Power Plant involving the retraction of a stuck source range monitor (SRM) from the reactor vessel. The first violation involved the failure to perform an evaluation of the potential radiological hazards associated with the work activity, as required by 10 CFR 20.1501. The second violation involved the failure to perform a complete radiological characterization of the SRM, as required by Technical Specification 5.7.1.b. The third violation involved the failure to establish a procedure that addressed the control of highly radioactive materials removed from the reactor vessel, as well as, the failure to implement a procedure to ensure that the licensee's ALARA plan contained steps to ensure that the ambient radiation field in the work areas were being controlled and that the workers actions were in accordance with ALARA considerations, as required by Technical Specification 5.4.1.

Nebraska Public Power District   EA-11-024
Cooper Nuclear Station

On June 10, 2011, an NOV was issued to Nebraska Public Power District for a violation of 10 CFR 50, Appendix B, Criterion XVI, "Corrective Action," and Criterion V, "Instructions, Procedures, and Drawings" identified as a result of an inspection at the Cooper Nuclear Station. The violation was associated with a White SDP finding involving the failure to establish measures to assure a condition adverse to quality was corrected and ensure the activities affecting quality were prescribed by documented procedures appropriate to the circumstances. Specifically, a violation issued on June 13, 2008, identified a condition adverse to quality in that two procedures would not work as written. While correcting that violation, the licensee failed to perform sufficient evaluation of the circuits to identify and correct a problem with three motor-operated valves needed to establish core cooling. Failure to correct the condition adverse to quality resulted in inadequate procedures in that they contained steps that were inappropriate to the circumstances because they would not work as written to reposition the three motor-operated valves.

Northern States Power Company   EA-11-110
Prairie Island Nuclear Generating Plant

On August 17, 2011, an NOV was issued to Northern States Power Company for a violation associated with a White SDP Process finding identified as a result of an inspection at the Prairie Island Nuclear Generating Plant. The violation involved the failure to maintain the direct current electrical power subsystems operable in Modes 1 through 4, as required by Technical Specification 3.8.4. Specifically, from December 21, 1994 to approximately October 22, 2010, all battery chargers in Unit 1 were susceptible to a common mode failure under design basis accident conditions. Under those conditions, the battery chargers would stop providing an output, or "lock-up," when their alternating current input voltage dropped below their nameplate minimum voltage at the battery charger motor control center.

Omaha Public Power District   EA-11-025
Fort Calhoun Station

On July 18, 2011, an NOV was issued to Omaha Public Power District for a violation of 10 CFR 50, Appendix B, Criterion XVI, "Corrective Action," identified as a result of an inspection at the Fort Calhoun Station. The violation was associated with a White SDP finding involving the failure to assure that the cause of a significant condition adverse to quality was determined and corrective actions taken to preclude repetition. Specifically, between November 3, 2008 and June 14, 2010, the licensee failed to preclude shading coils from repetitively becoming loose material in the M2 reactor trip contactor. The licensee failed to identify that the loose parts in the trip contactor represented a potential failure of the contactor if they became an obstruction and therefore, failed to preclude repetition of this significant condition adverse to quality, that subsequently resulted in the contactor failing.

Progress Energy   EA-11-208
Crystal River Nuclear Plant

On December 20, 2011, an NOV was issued to Progress Energy for a violation of 10 CFR 50.54(q) identified as a result of an inspection at the Crystal River Nuclear Plant. The violation was associated with a White SDP finding involving the failure of Crystal River personnel to maintain in effect a standard emergency classification scheme that included facility effluent parameters. Specifically, for several years prior to June 2011, the General Emergency classification contained effluent radiation monitors threshold values greater than those that the instruments could accurately measure. During an actual emergency, these monitors would have been relied upon to determine initial offsite response measures, to assess the impact of the release of radioactive materials, and to provide criteria for determining the need for notification and participation of local and State agencies.

Southern California Edison Company   EA-11-083
San Onofre Nuclear Generating Station

On August 4, 2011, an NOV was issued to Southern California Edison Company for a Severity Level III violation identified as a result of an inspection at the San Onofre Nuclear Generating Station. The violation involved the failure to certify that the qualifications and status of a senior operator licensee were current and valid and that the senior operator licensee had completed a minimum of 40 hours of shift functions under the direction of an operator or senior operator, as required by 10 CFR 55.53(e) and (f). Specifically, on October 21 and October 27, 2010, the licensee did not certify that qualifications of the senior operator licensee were current and valid and scheduled the senior operator to perform licensed activities (core alterations) as refueling senior operator supervisor while his license was INACTIVE. Additionally, the senior operator was not medically qualified in accordance with ANSI 3.4 (1996) to perform licensed duties.

Tennessee Valley Authority   EA-11-018
Browns Ferry Nuclear Power Plant

On May 9, 2011, an NOV was issued to Tennessee Valley Authority for a violation associated with a Red SDP finding identified as a result of an inspection at the Browns Ferry Nuclear Power Plant. The violation involved the failure to implement an In-Service Testing program in accordance with the American Society of Mechanical Engineers, Code for Operation and Maintenance of Nuclear Power Plants, 1995 Edition, 1996 Addenda, Section ISTC 4.1. Specifically, the inadequacy of TVA's programs resulted in the Unit 1 LPCI outboard injection valve, 1-FCV-74-66, being left in a significantly degraded condition and the Unit 1 LPCI/RHR Loop II unable to fulfill its safety function. (See Section II of this report for additional information).

Notices Issued To Material Licensees

Associated Specialists, Inc.   EA-11-179
Bridgeport, WV

On September 21, 2011, an NOV was issued to Associated Specialists, Inc. (ASI), for a Severity Level III problem involving two violations. The first violation involved the failure to limit operation with a temporary radiation safety officer (RSO) to a period of 60 days, as required by 10 CFR 35.24(c). The second violation involved the failure to ensure that an authorized user provided adequate supervision to licensee staff who were involved in the receipt, possession, use, transfer or preparation of byproduct material, as required by 10 CFR 35.27.

Bristol Hospital, Inc.   EA-11-008
Bristol, CT

On February 17, 2011, an NOV was issued to Bristol Hospital, Inc for a Severity Level III violation involving the failure to notify the NRC Operations Center of two medical events as required by 10 CFR 35.3045(c). Specifically, on January 12, 2010, Bristol Hospital experienced two medical events involving patients receiving less than the intended prescribed dose during two different permanent prostrate brachytherapy seed implants. The licensee should have reported the events to the NRC by March 2, 2010, but did not do so until June 2, 1010.

Cardinal Health PET Manufacturing Services, Inc.   EA-11-146
Dublin, OH

On November 9, 2011, an NOV was issued to Cardinal Health PET Manufacturing Services, Inc for a Severity Level III violation involving the failure to monitor the occupational exposure to an adult who was likely to receive, in one year from sources external to the body, an extremity dose in excess of 5 rem as required by 10 CFR 20.1502(a)(1). Specifically, on June 16, 2010, a Cardinal Health PET Manufacturing Services employee removed his extremity (ring) dosimetry on two separate occasions prior to handling a chemical cartridge containing approximately 4 curies of fluorine-18.

Carmeuse Lime, Inc.   EA-11-145
River Rouge, MI

On September 2, 2011, an NOV was issued to Carmeuse Lime, Inc. for a Severity Level III Problem involving three violations. The first violation involved the failure to have an individual specifically authorized to fulfill the duties and responsibilities as the Radiation Safety Officer (RSO) as required by Condition 12.A of the license. Specifically, the specified RSO left the company in 2007, and the licensee failed to appoint a new RSO and amend its license. The second violation involved the failure to conduct a physical inventory every six months, or at other intervals approved by the NRC, to account for all sealed sources and devices received and possessed under the license as required by Condition 15 of the license. The third violation involved the failure to test each gauge for the proper operation of the on-off mechanism (shutter) and indicator, if any, at intervals not to exceed six months or at intervals specified in the certificate of registration as required by Condition 16.B of the license.

Charleston Radiation Therapy Consultants, PLLC   EA-11-115
Charleston, WV

On June 30, 2011, an NOV was issued to Charleston Radiation Therapy Consultants, PLLC (CRTC) for a Severity Level III violation involving the failure to meet the physical presence requirements of 10 CFR 35.615(f)(2) during high dose radiation (HDR) treatments. Specifically, on an indeterminate number of occasions on and prior to April 28, 2011, neither a CRTC authorized user (AU), nor a physician under the supervision of an AU, was physically present during continuation of patient treatments involving the HDR unit.

Community Hospitals of Indiana   EA-11-016
Indianapolis, IN

On April 20, 2011, an NOV was issued to the Community Hospitals of Indiana for a Severity Level III violation involving the failure to fully implement procedures to provide high confidence that a brachytherapy treatment was in accordance with the written directive as required by 10 CFR 35.41(a). Specifically, on September 30, 2010, an authorized medical physicist missed a step in the procedure that established the starting position for the high dose remote afterloader brachytherapy treatment. The failure to implement this step resulted in a medical event.

Crittenton Hospital   EA-11-165
Rochester, MI

On September 2, 2011, an NOV was issued to Crittenton Hospital for a Severity Level III violation involving the failure to develop written procedures to provide high confidence that each administration was in accordance with the written directive as required by 10 CFR 35.41(a). Specifically, between September 2009 and January 2011, the licensee failed to address in its written procedure the need to verify that the step size used in the treatment plan was correctly translated into the high dose rate remote afterloader unit. As a result, the device's control unit default step size of 2.5 mm was used instead of the 5 mm used in the treatment planning system.

Del Valle Group   EA-11-009
Toa Baja, PR

On May 11, 2011, an NOV was issued to Del Valle Group (DVG) for a Severity Level III violation involving the failure to obtain authorization in a specific NRC license to own and possess three portable moisture density gauges as required by 10 CFR 30.3(a). Specifically, from November 30, 2008 through October 28, 2010, DVG owned or possessed byproduct material (discrete radium-226 sources contained in three portable moisture density gauges) without authorization in a specific or general license issued in accordance with NRC regulations.

Escanaba Paper Company   EA-11-061
Escanaba, MI

October 17, 2011, an NOV was issued to Escanaba Paper Company for a Severity Level III violation involving the failure to ensure that only persons specifically licensed by the NRC or an Agreement State perform services involving the dismantling and non-routine maintenance or repair of components related to the radiological safety of a gauge containing licensed material. Specifically, on May 9, 2011, the licensee performed non-routine maintenance on a fixed level gauge by using a rod to change the position of the shutter contrary to NRC License No. 21-17630-01, Condition 17.B. The licensee was not specifically licensed by the NRC or an Agreement State to perform this service.

Henry Ford Macomb Hospital   EA-11-088
Clinton Township, MI

On June 24, 2011, an NOV was issued to Henry Ford Macomb Hospital for a Severity Level III violation involving the failure to develop, implement, and maintain written procedures to provide high confidence that each administration is in accordance with the written directive as required by 10 CFR 35.41(a). Specifically, as of December 9, 2010, the licensee's procedure did not include steps to verify that the transfer tube assembly used at the time of the administration was the same length as the one identified in the treatment plan implementing the written directive. This resulted in four patients receiving radiation doses to areas not included within the planned treatment area.

Liberty Hospital   EA-11-109
Liberty, MO

On July 22, 2011, an NOV was issued to Liberty Hospital for a Severity Level III violation involving the failure to develop, implement, and maintain written procedures to provide high confidence that each administration was in accordance with the written directive as required by 10 CFR 35.41(a). Specifically, as of October 6, 2010, the licensee's procedure did not require the position of the prostate to be verified prior to seed placement. As a result, the prostate received a dose of 16.9 Gray (Gy) as opposed to the prescribed dose of 125 Gy.

Mercy Hospital   EA-11-094
Muskegon, MI

On June 8, 2011, an NOV was issued to Mercy Hospital for a Severity Level III violation involving the failure to develop, implement, and maintain written procedures to provide high confidence that each administration is in accordance with the written directive as required by 10 CFR 35.41(a). Specifically, between June 18, 2008 and February 23, 2011, the licensee performed approximately 200 high dose-rate (HDR) remote afterloader administrations requiring written directives and failed to develop written procedures to provide high confidence that each administration was in accordance with the written directive.

Oakwood Hospital – Annapolis Center   EA-11-010
Wayne, MI

On March 4, 2011, an NOV was issued to Oakwood Hospital – Annapolis Center for a Severity Level III problem involving two violations. The first violation involved the failure to ensure that an administered dose did not differ from the prescribed dose by more than 20 percent as required by 10 CFR 35.63(d). The second violation involved the failure to verify that the assayed dosage was within 10 percent of the prescribed activity as required by License Condition 15.A. Specifically, the licensee administered approximately 124.5 millicuries of sodium pertechnetate technetium-99m (Tc-99m) to a patient instead of the prescribed dosage of 10 millicuries of Tc-99m tetrofosmin, a difference in excess of 20 percent. The licensee also failed to verify that it had the correct syringe, which resulted in the incorrect radiopharmaceutical and dosage being administered to the patient.

Owensby and Kritikos, Inc.   EA-11-100
Gretna, LA

On June 8, 2011, an NOV was issued to Owensby and Kritikos, Inc., for a Severity Level III violation involving the licensee's failure to control and maintain constant surveillance of licensed material in an unrestricted area as required by 10 CFR 20.1801 and 20.1802. Specifically, on July 29, 2010, a radiography camera containing licensed radioactive material was found on the floor of an unlocked darkroom and no radiography personnel were maintaining constant surveillance over the material.

Providence Hospital   EA-11-037
Southfield, MI

On May 17, 2011, an NOV was issued to Providence Hospital for a Severity Level III violation involving the failure to develop, implement, and maintain written procedures to provide high confidence that each administration was in accordance with the written directive as required by 10 CFR 35.41(a). Specifically, as of August 30, 2010, the licensee's brachytherapy procedure did not provide high confidence that the needles would be inserted to the right depth as the licensee did not require the use of available means such as biological or needle markers.

U. S. Department of the Army   EA-10-129
Arlington, VA

On August 1, 2011, an NOV was issued to the U. S. Department of the Army (Army) for a Severity Level III violation involving the failure to have authorization in a specific or general license to possess depleted uranium (DU), a source material in quantities in excess of the exempt and general use limits, as required by10 CFR 40.3. Specifically, from April 1978, when NRC license SUB-459 expired, to August 2011, the Army continued to possess DU associated with the Davy Crockett weapons system in the form of spent fragments of spotting rounds (obtained from 1962 to 1968, and expended prior to 1968) at firing ranges located at the Army's two installations in Hawaii; Schofield Barracks and Pohakuloa Training Area. In addition to the two installations in Hawaii, the Army has also identified the presence of spent DU spotting rounds at other Army installations across the United States.

Warner Brothers, LLC   EA-11-209
East Deerfield, MA

On November 8, 2011, an NOV was issued to Warner Brothers, LLC for a Severity Level III violation involving the failure to file NRC Form 241 "Report of Proposed Activities in Non-Agreement States," at least three days prior to engaging in licensed activities within NRC jurisdiction as required by 10 CFR 150.20. Specifically, on December 6, 2006, and July 7, 2008, Warner Brothers LLC, which only holds a Massachusetts (an agreement state) license, used a portable gauge containing a sealed source, at temporary jobsites within the State of Connecticut (a non-agreement state), without obtaining a specific license issued by the NRC or filing NRC Form-241 with the NRC.

West Virginia University Hospitals, Inc.   EA-11-027
Morgantown, WV

On March 25, 2011, an NOV was issued to West Virginia University Hospitals Inc. (WVUH) for a Severity Level III violation involving the failure to notify the NRC Operations Center by telephone no later than the next calendar day after discovery of a medical event as required by 10 CFR 35.3045(c). Specifically, WVUH did not notify the NRC until July 7, 2010, after discovering that a dose administered on January 20, 2010 differed from the prescribed dose.

William Beaumont Hospital   EA-11-163
Royal Oak, MI

On September 2, 2011, an NOV was issued to William Beaumont Hospital for a Severity Level III violation involving the failure to develop, implement, and maintain written procedures to provide high confidence that each administration was in accordance with the written directive as required by 10 CFR 35.41(a). Specifically, as of May 5, 2011, the licensee's written procedures for yttrium-90 treatments did not specify how personnel should administer a treatment using a fine bore catheter and a high concentration of microspheres in order to prevent blockage within the catheter.

Notices Issued To Fuel Cycle Licensees

Westinghouse Electric Company (Commercial Nuclear Fuels Division)   EA-10-153
Columbia, SC

On February 25, 2011, an NOV was issued to Westinghouse Electric Company, Commercial Nuclear Fuel Division, for a Severity Level III problem involving three violations associated with the Integral Fuel Burnable Absorber (IFBA) Filter Press used in the waste water handling system. The first violation involved the failure to establish double contingency for the IFBA filter press to protect against an inadvertent criticality as required by License Condition 6.1.1. The second violation involved the failure to designate items relied on for safety (IROFS) to limit the risk of a high consequence event as required by 10 CFR 70.61(e). The third violation involved the failure to designate the passive engineered controls of the IFBA filter press as an IROFS as required by the license and license application based on the conclusion that the accident scenario was not credible. In addition, two Severity Level IV violations were issued involving the failure to establish adequate operating procedures for the filter press and the failure to make a change to facility equipment in accordance with approved procedures. These violations existed on and before July 23, 2010.

Appendix C: Summary of Orders[*]

Orders Issued To Reactor Licensees

Entergy Operations, Inc.   EA-11-096
River Bend Station

On August 24, 2011, an Immediately Effective Confirmatory Order was issued to Entergy Nuclear Operations Inc. and Entergy Operations Inc. (Entergy) to formalize commitments made as a result of an ADR mediation session held on July 18, 2011. By letter dated May 20, 2011, the NRC identified an apparent violation of 10 CFR 50.7 to Entergy based on the NRC's Office of Investigations, March 17, 2011 report (OI Case No. 4-2010-053). Specifically, the NRC had reached a preliminary conclusion that an employee at the River Bend Station was rated lower in their 2008 annual performance appraisal based in part on the employee questioning the qualifications necessary to perform certain work activities in compliance with applicable plant procedures.

Prior to the issuance of the NRC's May 20, 2011 letter but following a separate NRC inquiry, Entergy conducted its own internal investigation of the circumstances giving rise to the apparent violation. The NRC recognized that as a result of its investigation, Entergy took several specific actions at the River Bend Station and several fleet-wide actions. The fleet-wide actions included conducting supervisory and Employee Concerns Program personnel training on 10 CFR 50.7; reviewing all closed internal retaliation type cases in 2008 and 2009; reviewing all 2009 appraisals for employees with overall "improvement required" rating; and revising several quality-affecting procedures.

As a result of the settlement agreement from the ADR mediation session, Entergy agreed to take a number of additional fleet-wide actions. A summary of those fleet-wide actions are: (1) reorganizing the quality control organization's reporting structure; (2) reinforcing the company's commitment to a safety conscious work environment through a written communication from a senior Entergy nuclear executive; (3) reviewing and, as necessary, revising the existing general employee training on 10 CFR 50.7 to include insights from the circumstances giving rise to this matter; (4) reviewing and, as necessary, revising training to new supervisors for 10 CFR 50.7 to include insights from the circumstances giving rise to this matter; and (5) conducting an effectiveness review of the Employee Concerns Program enhancements and training that were implemented relating to the underlying matter. Entergy also agreed to conduct a plant wide safety culture survey at the River Bend Station prior to December 31, 2012.

In recognition of Entergy's prior actions and in exchange for the additional actions Entergy agreed to take as described in the enclosed confirmatory order, the NRC agreed not to pursue further action relating to this matter which may have otherwise resulted in the issuance of a Notice of Violation with a base civil penalty had it not reached a settlement agreement.

---

[*] *Please note that cases involving security-related issues are not included*

Orders Issued To Material Licensees

Four Confirmatory Orders issued to Material Licensees involved civil penalties and are discussed in Appendix A.

Orders Issued To Fuel Cycle Licensees

United States Enrichment Corporation   EA-11-056
Paducah Facility

On August 17, 2011, an Immediately Effective Confirmatory Order was issued to the United States Enrichment Corporation (USEC) to confirm commitments made as a result of an ADR mediation session held on July 22, 2011. This enforcement action is based on a violation involving an incident in which an operator deliberately violated applicable radiation protection procedures. Specifically, the violation involved the failure to adhere to the requirements of a USEC Paducah procedure that requires personnel to perform a whole body frisk when exiting from areas controlled for removable contamination. USEC agreed to take a number of actions including (1) conducting a prompt investigation into the incident; (2) conducting multiple staff briefings by USEC-Paducah management, procedural reviews and revisions as warranted, appropriate retraining and communicating lessons learned to staff; (3) reviewing the circumstances that took place during the routine operational activities that resulted in the existence of contaminated material; and (4) taking disciplinary action against the employee involved in the incident. In addition, USEC committed to enhancing new employee orientation and General Employee Training at Paducah to ensure that personnel clearly understand the consequences of deliberate acts of non-compliance with regulations or procedures, and expanding its independent, Safety Conscious Work Environment assessment to include an assessment of the safety culture components of decision making and work practices. In recognition of USEC's proposed extensive corrective actions, in addition to corrective actions already taken, the NRC agreed to not issue a Notice of Violation, and refrain from proposing a civil penalty for this matter.

Orders Issued To Individuals

Gregory Desobry   IA-10-010

On February 23, 2011, an Order was issued to Mr. Gregory Desobry requiring him to notify the NRC prior to any future involvement in NRC licensed or Agreement State regulated activities This enforcement action was taken in order to provide the NRC with an opportunity to verify the effectiveness of corrective actions that Mr. Desobry has taken in response to his involvement in the medical events that occurred at the VA Philadelphia Medical Center from February 2002 through June 2008 (EA-09-038). Specifically, the Order requires Mr. Desobry to make a one-time notification to the NRC within 20 days of his accepting employment as a medical physicist in NRC licensed or Agreement State regulated activities. The Order noted that Mr. Desobry provided a description of the corrective actions he had taken in a June 28, 2010 reply to a Demand for Information that the NRC issued on May 24, 2010.

Gary Kao   IA-09-035

On February 23, 2011, an Order prohibiting involvement in NRC licensed activities was issued to Dr. Gary Kao. This enforcement action was taken in order to provide the NRC with reasonable assurance that the protection of public health and safety will not be compromised until such time that Dr. Kao provides NRC with sufficient information relative to the corrective actions he has taken to address his part in the medical events that occurred at the VA Philadelphia Medical Center from February 2002 through June 2008 (EA-09-038). Specifically, the Order prohibits Dr. Kao's involvement in any NRC licensed activity until rescinded by the NRC, contingent upon Dr. Kao's completing specialized training, demonstrating the ability to correctly identify and report medical events, and providing other documentation to the NRC supporting completion of the requirements specified in the Order. The Order noted that Dr. Kao voluntarily stopped performing brachytherapy treatments and committed to take all necessary and appropriate steps to ensure that he was current on all applicable requirements should he perform brachytherapy treatments in the future.

Action Involving the Atomic Safety and Licensing Board Panel

Mattingly Testing Services, Inc.   EA-10-100
Molt, MT

On September 2, 2010 the NRC issued two orders: (1) an order revoking the license of Mattingly Testing Services, Inc. (MTS) (EA-10-100); and (2) an order to Mark M. Ficek prohibiting involvement in NRC-licensed activities (IA-10-028). In response to these orders, two employees of MTS requested a hearing. After submitting the hearing requests, the NRC staff entered into settlement negotiations with the parties, and on February 22, 2011, an NRC Atomic Safety and Licensing Board (ASLB) issued a Memorandum and Order (Order) accepting the settlement and dismissing the hearing proceeding. Specifically, the NRC staff and two parties, employees of MTS agreed to a settlement on February 4, 2011, in lieu of continuing the hearing proceeding. The Settlement Agreement was forwarded to the ASLB and approved. The February 22, 2011 Order superseded the September 2, 2010 Order issued to MTS and the Order issued to Mark M. Ficek. The approved settlement included the following terms and conditions: (1) the MTS license remains revoked and parties agree that it will not be reinstated; (2) Mr. Ficek is prohibited from engaging in NRC-licensed activities until September 2, 2017 (the settlement further defines NRC-licensed activities); (3) for a three year period after September 2, 2017, Mr. Ficek is required to notify NRC of employment involving NRC-licensed activities; (4) Mr. Ficek is allowed non-controlling ownership in an NRC licensee, subject to conditions specified in the settlement prohibiting Mr. Ficek's engagement in licensed activities; (5) Mr. Ficek is allowed to own and/or sell the radiographic exposure devices that were listed on the former MTS license, subject to conditions specified in the settlement; and, (6) all parties agree that all further procedural steps before the ASLB and any right to challenge or contest the validity of the Order entered into in accordance with the Settlement Agreement, and all rights to seek judicial review or otherwise contest the validity of the Order are expressly waived.

Appendix D: Summary of Escalated Enforcement Actions against Individuals[*]

Orders

Two Orders were issued to individuals during 2011 and are discussed in Appendix C.

An Atomic and Safety Licensing Board Settlement Agreement Order involving an individual is also discussed in Appendix C.

Notices of Violation

Christopher A. Moore   IA-11-037

On November 9, 2011, an NOV was issued to Christopher A. Moore, former Radiation Safety Officer at Cardinal Health PET Manufacturing Services, Inc., in St. Louis, Missouri, for a Severity Level III violation involving 10 CFR 30.10, "Deliberate Misconduct." Specifically, on June 16, 2010, Mr. Moore caused Cardinal Health PET Manufacturing Services, Inc., an applicant for an NRC license, to be in violation of 10 CFR 20.1502(a)(1) which requires that a licensee (in this case, an applicant) monitor the occupational exposure to adults likely to receive, in one year from sources external to the body, a dose in excess of 10 percent of the limits in 10 CFR 20.1201(a). The nature of Mr. Moore's position made him subject to 10 CFR 20.1502(a)(1). However, Mr. Moore deliberately removed his extremity (ring) dosimetry on two separate occasions prior to handling a chemical cartridge containing approximately 4 curies of fluorine-18.

Craig M. Rice   IA-11-056

On September 21, 2011, an NOV was issued to Mr. Craig M. Rice, formerly a licensed reactor operator at the Fermi Power Plant, Unit No. 2, for a Severity Level III violation involving the failure to comply with the requirements of 10 CFR 55.53(j). Specifically, on April 25, 2011, Mr. Rice participated in the Detroit Edison Company random fitness for duty testing program and subsequently tested positive for an illegal substance.

Roger A. Shaffer   IA-11-012

On March 18, 2011, an NOV was issued to Mr. Roger A. Shaffer, formerly a licensed reactor operator at the Palisades Nuclear Plant, Unit No. 1, for a SLIII violation involving the failure to comply with the requirements of 10 CFR 55.53(j). Specifically, on December 20, 2010, Mr. Shaffer participated in the Entergy Nuclear Operations, Inc. random fitness for duty testing program and subsequently tested positive for an illegal substance.

---

[*] *Please note that cases involving security-related issues are not included*

Appendix E: Summary of Escalated Enforcement Actions against Nonlicensees (Vendors, Contractors and Certificate Holders)[*]

Notice of Violation

Carro & Carro Enterprises, Inc.   EA-10-272
Ciales, PR

On February 11, 2011, a Notice of Violation was issued to Carro & Carro Enterprises, Inc. (CCE) for a Severity Level III violation involving the failure to obtain authorization in a specific NRC license to own and possess a portable moisture density gauge, which contained byproduct material. Specifically, from November 30, 2008, through June 28, 2009, CCE owned or possessed byproduct material, a discrete radium-226 source contained in a portable moisture density gauge, without authorization in a specific or general license issued in accordance with NRC regulations.

---

[*] *Please note that cases involving security-related issues are not included*